Patchwork Patterns

To Donna,
Best Wishes,
Jinny Beyer
San Luis Obispo, Calif.
Sept. 1984

Patchwork Patterns

For all crafts that use geometric design— quilting, stained glass, mosaics, graphics, needlepoint, jewelry, weaving and woodworking.

Jinny Beyer

EPM PUBLICATIONS, INC.

EPM Publications, Inc. 1003 Turkey Run Road, McLean, Virginia 22101
Printed in the United States of America

Library of Congress Cataloging in Publication Data

Beyer, Jinny.
    Patchwork patterns.
    Includes index.
    1. Patchwork—Patterns.   I. Title.

TT835.B43   745.4   78-32055

Patchwork Patterns is published simultaneously in hard and soft cover.

ISBN 0-914440-26-8 hard cover
ISBN 0-914440-27-6 soft cover

Illustrations by Jinny Beyer and Dan Ramsey

Cover: *Ray of Light,* pieced medallion quilt by Jinny Beyer
        Photograph by Roy Hale

Design by Gerard A. Valerio

Contents

Acknowledgments

Until one has embarked on a project such as this, it is impossible to know the amount of work involved. I am thankful to my husband, John, and to our three children Sean, Darren and Kiran for putting up with all the chaos during the writing of this book.

I wish to thank Steve Thompson who did the photography, and those people who allowed me to use photographs of their quilts. I also want to thank my sister, Wendy Kahle, for her drawing and Homer Smith who explained to me the technique discussed in Chapter III and Peter Kramer whose furniture appears in the color photographs.

A very special thanks goes to Dan Ramsey who literally worked night and day to finish the illustrations. Without his help and his artistic talents, this book would not have been what it is.

JINNY BEYER

I want to dedicate this work to all my students. Without them this book would have never happened. Each time I teach a class on pattern drafting, I also learn something new from my students and many of them have contributed to the content of this book.

A Word to All Pattern Drafters

The past ten years have seen a remarkable renewal of interest in our heritage. The renaissance of "craft art" has been astounding. One does not need to look far to discover an excellent woodworker, potter or needleworker.

With the revival of crafts has come a great interest in quilts and geometric patchwork designs. It is not only the quilter who is interested. Craftsmen in many other fields such as stained glass, needlepoint and graphic art are also using patchwork designs in their work.

This book is written for those who have an interest in using traditional geometric designs or a desire to create their own original motifs.

Too often people give up on designs they wish to do because they cannot find a pattern for it. They search through book after book hoping to find the right-sized block. The rare articles that explain how to draft patterns often confuse rather than help people. Graph paper, complicated formulas, Pythagorean theorems, square roots: There seems to be a need to be a mathematical genius as well as a craftsman!

There are many quilt books which give *patterns* for geometric patchwork designs, but there seem to be none that go into detail or are devoted entirely to drafting one's *own*. Thus the constant question: "Does anyone have a pattern for 'broken star,'" or "I am looking for an eight inch block of the 'log cabin,'" and so on.

It was a frustration with mathematics, a loathing of the tedious process of enlarging squares, a desire to have any pattern of any size when I wanted it—not when I could find it in a book—and a wish to develop new designs that led to my experimentation with paper-folding and finally to a system for drafting almost any geometric patchwork pattern. I would like to note, however, that this system must be similar to that used by many women in the 19th century. Some of their quilt patterns were published in newspapers and periodicals of the time, others were passed down from one woman to the next, but still new ones and adaptations were developed. Some women must have followed a paper-folding procedure for drafting many of their designs.

My purpose in this book is not to introduce some "new and amazing" technique, but to explain in a systematic manner a method of drafting patterns which has, in large, been put aside, and about which no comprehensive book has been written. I will also explain a few simple drafting techniques which are particularly useful in making geometric designs. Even though I have approached this book as a quilter, the same methods described here can be used by craftsmen in other fields who have a need for geometric designs.

I have not written about combining fabrics in this book. However, I have tried to put textures together in the illustrations in a manner that I might use if I were sewing the design. A study of the illustrations will give you more ideas on fabric use than a written explanation would.

Throughout the book I will be making statements about the way I do various aspects of quilting, designing and drafting. I would like to emphasize that I do not believe that my way of doing things is the "only" or the "right" way. One of the exciting things about quiltmaking is its versatility. Ten people can begin with the same pattern and create ten totally different quilts by varying the color, fabric, borders or proportions of the design. And all ten can each have a beautiful creation.

The whole concept of pattern drafting lies in the ability to be able to look at a geometric design and classify it into its proper category. Once that category is identified, one can then fold a square of paper into the basic "grid" for that category. Once the paper has been folded, it is then possible, with the aid of a ruler and/or a few additional folds, to make all the pattern pieces necessary for that particular design.

This book categorizes geometric patterns, shows the folding and drafting methods for the designs in each category and also explains a method for dividing a square into any number of equal units.

It is important to read the book from the beginning because it moves step by step and each chapter gives information which will help in the next. In order to benefit from the book, sit down with some paper squares, a ruler and a pencil, and work out the patterns each step of the way. Test yourself. Turn to page 194 and see how many of the designs you can draft. After reading Chapter I, look at the designs again and see if you can tell which categories they fall into. After studying the book try again and check your results with the answers on page 196. The only way to learn is by doing.

With some diligent study of what is offered in these pages, I feel any craftsman will have the ability to draft whatever geometric designs he or she chooses.

Patchwork Patterns

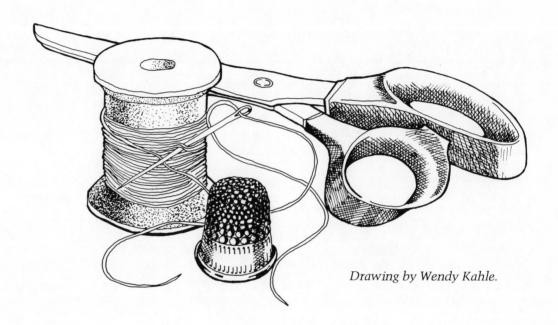

Drawing by Wendy Kahle.

CHAPTER I

Getting Started

Before starting on pattern drafting, one has to have an idea of the methods of piecing, the types of projects and the scope of design he or she wishes to use. It is important to note that the manner in which the patches are sewn together will, in some respects, determine the type of pattern which should be chosen.

When drafting a design keep in mind whether or not you are going to piece by hand or by machine. The more intricate patterns such as the *Sunburst,* and any that have angles which are to be set in, such as *Grandmother's Flower Garden,* are very difficult to piece with perfection on the sewing machine. One of the first things I teach in my classes is that for the work to look right, *the points must meet.* If the piecing is to be done by machine, it is important to look for patterns which can be put together in units using all straight seams. If the pattern has an angle to set in, try to revise it so that it can be sewn in straight lines or sew the pieces by hand.

I piece all of my quilts by hand, but use the machine for some of my other projects. To me quilts are special. I like to do intricate piecing and fairly complicated designs which I cannot do well on the machine. It is easier to get tiny points to meet by hand than by machine.

The sewing machine gives me a completely different feeling from the relaxation I get with handwork. I have made clothes for years and to me making a dress means cutting it out in the morning, sewing it during the day and wearing it that night. When it comes to machine work, I cannot escape the "rush" syndrome. Machine work also puts me in isolation. I cannot talk to or be with my family as I can when I do handwork.

There are many patchwork projects that I do make on the sewing machine. Since it takes close to a year to complete a quilt by hand, there are times when I need some instant gratification. I can get that from making patchwork clothes, pillows, Christmas presents and other items that will be out of style soon or will wear out quickly with use.

When you piece by hand, there is no rush to finish. Every step of the way is savored like a gourmet meal with each part enjoyed for what it is and satisfaction taken over each piece finished. The quilt is full of memories because you can take the piecing with you. I can look at each of my quilts and remember the past through them — traveling to various parts of the world, sitting in the hospital with a sick child, Little League games and much more. Because it is viewed as a long-term project the work is done slowly, with precision, and pride is taken in every stitch.

The whole nature of today's existence says, "Run, Hurry!" Ours is the age of 10-speed bikes, racing cars, SSTs, rockets to the moon. And I seem to be running just as fast as anyone else. I think that is why I enjoy so much the short time I can find each day to sit and relax with my piecing. This will be my quilt to last a lifetime, I am in no hurry, I can catch my breath.

Many of my beginning students ask what kind of project they should start with. I say, "Start a quilt." I have seen too many people get bogged down with pillows and small projects and never get the courage to begin a quilt. I think it is important to give yourself a challenge. Of course there are exceptions. Those who have never done any sewing or other handwork should learn the basics first. But if you are the type of person who always has a project going, has done sewing, worked on long-term knitting or crocheting projects or have a love of other crafts, you are ready to accept a challenge. You only learn by *doing*. Don't pick a simple design that you will be uninspired by and soon get bored with. If you are excited by the project there will be more incentive to finish it. Even if the design is difficult, by the time two or three blocks have been pieced you will be an expert with that design and will have learned all the pitfalls. In the end you may even decide to discard those first blocks and chalk them up to a learning experience. Jump in with both feet and accept a challenge. By the time you start the next quilt, you will have the confidence to try something really fantastic!

Once a design is decided upon for a project the next task is to make templates. "Templates" are the patterns used when cutting out the fabric. However, unlike dress patterns, patchwork patterns should not be made out of paper, but sandpaper, sturdy cardboard, metal or clear plastic. The templates must be *exact;* if the pattern is off, it will throw the whole quilt off.

There are many patchwork pattern books available from which you could make templates. A problem arises, however, when a different size pattern is needed than that which is given in the book. There are so many uses for patchwork that you should be able to make a pattern any size: To fit a picture frame, the yoke of a dress, a purse, or any other project. Many times a block of a certain size is needed to fit a quilt. If a sampler quilt is being made, trying to find different patterns of the same size in all the quilting books could be an endless task. There is no longer a need to search. The tools needed are not calculators, protractors, slide rules, conversion charts and algebraic equations. All you need is the following:

Thin tracing paper
Sharp pencil or pen
Ruler
Draftsman's triangle (90° by 45° by 45°)
Scissors
Compass
Colored pencils or felt-tipped pens

A triangle is an excellent tool for pattern drafting. Most of all it can assure that you have perfect right angles. By lining one edge of it up with the base of the square, you can be absolutely sure that the sides are exactly perpendicular to the base line.

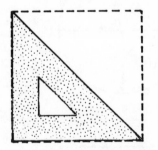

When experimenting with designs, any type of normal weight paper such as newsprint or typing paper can be used. When folding for a design to use for templates, use a very thin, but sturdy, tracing paper. If the paper is too heavy, accuracy will be lost because of the thickness of the folds. Bear in mind that it is not always necessary to fold the entire piece of paper. It is possible to cut out one section of the square after it has been divided into its basic units, and proceed from there. This can also insure accuracy by eliminating several more folds. A further explanation of this follows in succeeding chapters.

The first step is to decide what pattern you would like to draft (after reading this book you may decide to design your own pattern). Next decide what size block you want and make a square that size.

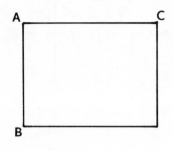

Making Squares

Most paper is rectangular. For practice and experimentation it does not matter what size square is used and it is easiest just to use tablet paper. To make a square out of a rectangle, simply fold line AB over to meet line AC and cut off the excess strip on the right.

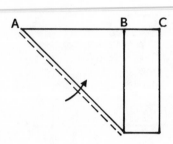

This simple method will give you a square that is good enough to play with but when drafting a pattern to use for actual templates it is extremely important that the square is *exact*. The corners must be true right angles. If the pattern is off, then the whole quilt will end up crooked and you will have nothing but grief in putting it together. Three ways to make a perfect square using a triangle will be discussed here.

Square Method I

1. Use a compass and draw a circle with the diameter the same size as the width of the square. If you want an 11″ square the diameter of the circle would be 11″ and the radius 5½″.

2. Place the triangle on the circle as in the diagram below so that one edge touches the right-hand side of of the circle and the other edge touches the top. Draw lines along the outer edges of the triangle.

3. Next place the triangle so that one edge matches the line at the top and the other edge touches the left side of the circle. Draw along the left edge.

4. Finally, place the triangle so one edge lies along the line just drawn and the other edge touches the bottom of the circle. Finish the square by drawing the last line.

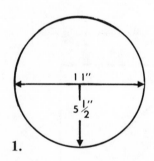

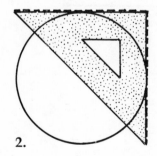

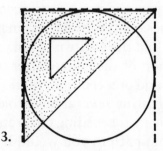

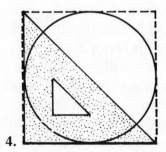

Square Method II

The second method of using a triangle to draft a square is very similar to the first. But this time a circle is not used.

1. Draw a straight line the width of the square.

2. Place the triangle along the line so the bottom edge is even with the line and the corner hits the end of the line.

   Draw a straight line up the side of the triangle the same length as the size of the square.

3. Repeat the process along the line just drawn to get the third side of the square.

4. Finish the square by connecting the top and bottom lines.

5. Using the right angle corner of the triangle double check all the corners of the square to be sure they are true right angles.

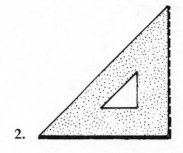

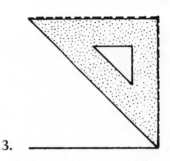

Square Method III

The third method for using a triangle to draft a square is a little different. Study the three methods and use the one which you find the easiest. Many times you may be working with an area where there is an odd-sized measurement. It might be 6⁷⁄₁₆″. This third method of drafting a square would be easiest to use in such situations because only one measurement—the base line of the square—needs to be made.

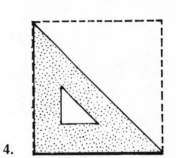

1. Draw a base line the width of the square and place the triangle on it so that one of the 45° angles touches the left side of the line (A). Draw a line diagonally up the long side of the triangle.

2. Turn the triangle over and place the sharp angle at B and draw a second diagonal line.

3. Next draw straight lines perpendicular to A and B using the triangle as explained on page 5.

4. Mark points C and D where the perpendicular lines meet the diagonal lines. By connecting C and D you will have a perfect square.

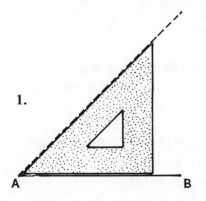

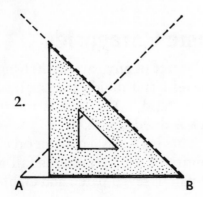

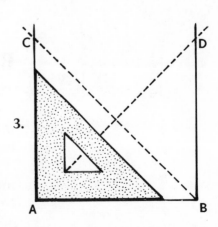

When determining what size block to make for the design, make the square the size of the entire *finished* block. Do *nothing* about seam allowances until the whole pattern is drafted, the individual shapes for the pattern pieces are cut, and you are ready to make the templates. Only then are seam allowances added *all the way around all sides of all pieces.* Many mistakes have been made when people have neglected to add seam allowances on all sides.

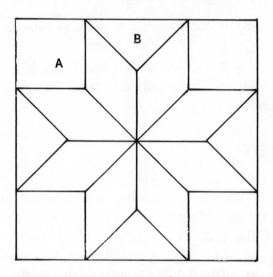

A very common mistake occurs when someone needs a square pattern piece "A" and a triangle "B" for the same pattern such as the eight-pointed star. In this particular design, pattern piece B is exactly half of A. After folding the pattern, the person cuts out the square, adds the seam allowance around all sides of it, and then cuts the square in half diagonally for the triangle. He then forgets to add the seam allowance along the edge just cut.

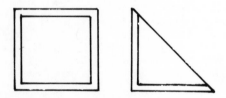

To avoid these pitfalls, wait until *all* shapes are cut out and then add the seam allowance around *all* sides of *all* pieces.

As the paper-folding methods are explained throughout the book, the center of the block will be marked with a dot. Keep this in mind as you fold and always be sure the center of your paper is in the same position as that on the diagram.

Basic Categories

The secret of any pattern drafting lies in being able to look at a pattern and divide it visually into units. Most designs fit into a "grid." The grid is the number of squares a pattern block is divided into.

This book has a chapter on each of the five categories the majority of square patterns fall into: Four-patch, nine-patch, five-patch, seven-patch and eight-pointed star.

Four-Patch

A four-patch is one that is divided into four squares. Don't be fooled. It can also be divided into multiples of four—16 squares, 64 squares, etc.

Nine-Patch

A nine-patch pattern has a grid of nine equal squares. It can be further divided into 36 squares.

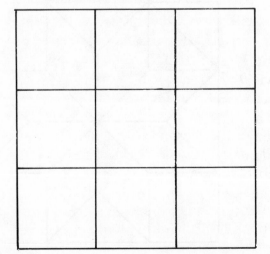
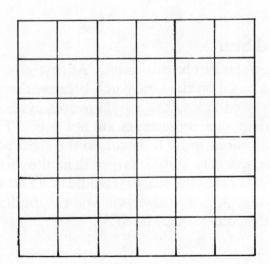

Five-Patch

Five-patch designs are ones in which the square is divided into twenty-five equal squares. For simplicity, rather than refer to these patterns as "twenty-five-patch," it is easier to call them "five-patch."

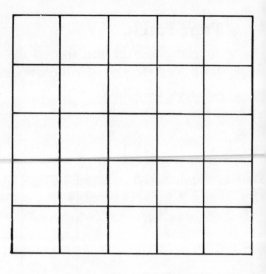

Seven-Patch

Seven-patch designs are those consisting of 49 squares. Again for simplicity it is easier to refer to these as seven-patch patterns, rather than forty-nine-patch.

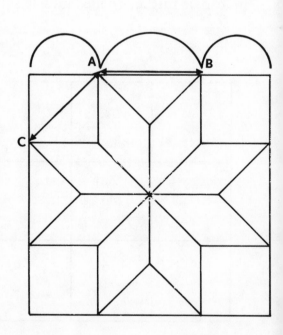

Eight-Pointed Star

The eight-pointed star can be misleading. At first glance one might think it is based on the nine-patch because three divisions are readily seen across the top. However, with closer study it is apparent that those units are not equal. To be a nine-patch the divisions *must* be equal. In the eight-pointed star, the middle space is always larger than the two side spaces. It is not two times the size or it would be a four-patch. The middle division (A to B) is always as wide as the diagonal distance across the corner square (C to A).

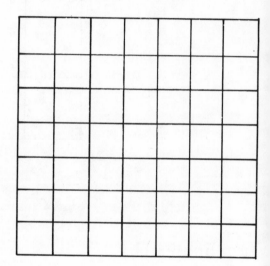

Others

Other smaller categories are five-pointed star, hexagon, curved patterns and patterns with isolated squares in the middle which are not related to any of the other categories.

All patterns will not necessarily have all the actual squares or divisions showing. It may be necessary to draw imaginary lines to see the divisions as in the diagrams below. The important thing is to be able *to see through* the design to the underlying grid. In many cases it is straightforward, but at times it takes more than a cursory glance to see the divisions. It may be necessary to take a pencil and actually draw the grid lines on the block.

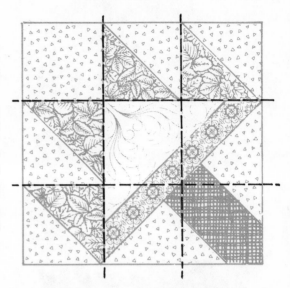

Graph paper is commonly used for drafting patchwork patterns and is probably the easiest method for some designs of certain sizes. Much of the information contained in this book works on the same principle as drafting on graph paper. With paper-folding and other techniques discussed here "grids" are created as on graph paper and then the squares are connected, diagonally and up and down, to get the different designs.

The problem with printed graph paper is that you are limited in the size of the square you can work with. It is easy to work with a size of block that fits within the grid of the graph paper; but when working with an odd-sized block such as 8¾″ or 11½″, it becomes more difficult to divide the square into thirds, fifths or sevenths. It is also difficult to use graph paper on five-pointed star, hexagon, circular, or eight-pointed star patterns. This is where paper-folding and the method for dividing a line into equal segments described in Chapter III are very useful.

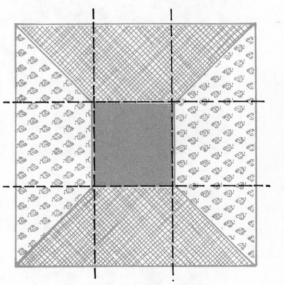

There are numerous diagrams of quilt patterns throughout this book. They are samples and meant to be used as a "guide" or key to understanding how to draft these and other patterns which have not been included.

If you can learn to master the folding and drafting techniques for the various categories, and can learn to identify patterns which fall into these categories, then you will be well on your way toward understanding pattern drafting and being able to make any pattern you choose.

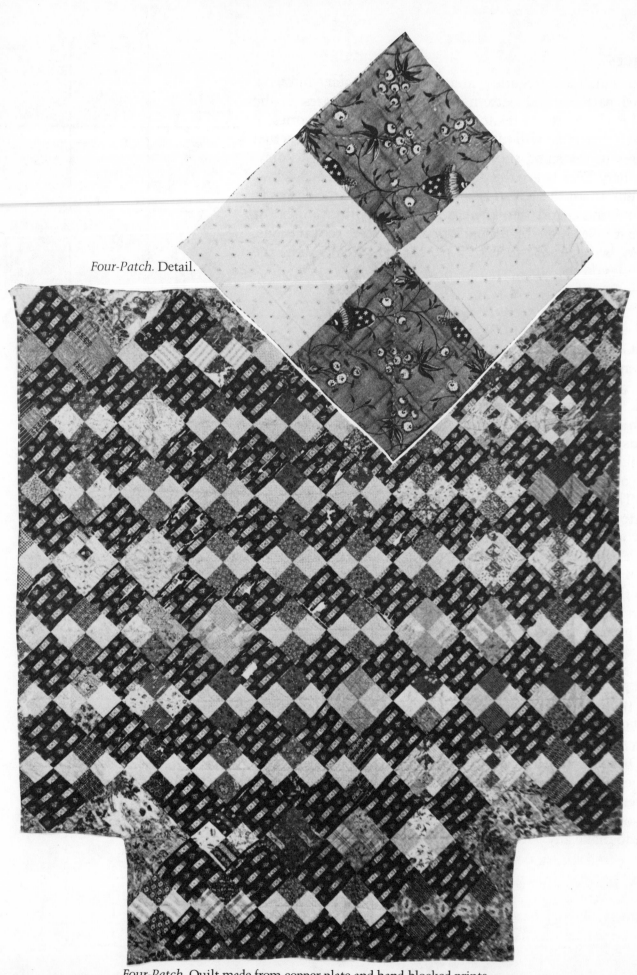

Four-Patch. Detail.

Four-Patch. Quilt made from copper plate and hand-blocked prints, circa 1790. Author's collection.

CHAPTER **II**

Four-Patch

The greatest number of quilt patterns seem to be derived from variations of the basic four-patch. Mention of this pattern to an old-time quilter will undoubtedly conjure up childhood memories of her first quilt which consisted of blocks made of four patches put together like a checkerboard.

This is the simplest form of square geometric design and the easiest to draft. Numerous designs grew from the four-patch. Many of these were most likely made by women folding squares into the basic four-patch division and then folding further to see what other designs could be created.

Construction of most four-patch patterns is relatively straightforward. It is simply a matter of making a "grid" of squares and then, by either folding or ruling, connecting the squares with lines to get the desired pattern.

Four-patch patterns are divided into three categories: The basic block divided into 1. four squares, 2. sixteen squares, or 3. sixty-four squares. Some designs will be a combination of these. A quarter of the design might be one large square, but another quarter might be 16 smaller squares. When working with a combination it will be necessary to construct a "grid" of the largest number of squares used in the block.

The easiest way to recognize the proper category is to count the divisions across the top of the block. Any time two, four or eight equal divisions can readily be seen, you know that it is a four-patch design, and you will be able to tell by the number of divisions which of the three categories it falls into.

I would like to note here that you will encounter designs where you can readily see the basic four squares of a four-patch such as *Rosebud* below. But in this case each quarter division is then broken down into thirds. Therefore instead of two, four or eight equal divisions across the top, there are six.

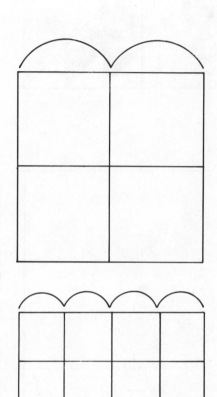

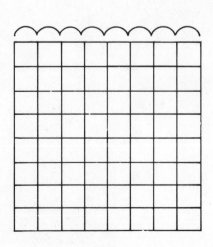

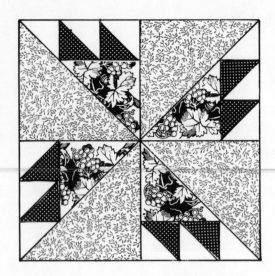

This design could not be drafted by repeatedly folding the paper in half. At some point it would have to be folded into thirds. Therefore, for simplicity of classifying and drafting, designs of this nature fall into the nine-patch category.

Four-patch designs are very easy to construct on graph paper if a size of block is desired that will easily fit into the squares of the paper. But if an odd-sized block is needed—one not in whole inches—then it is easier to construct the grid by folding the paper or by using one of the other methods discussed here.

Decide what size of block you want and make a square that size out of paper. Fold the square in half and then in half again. This will produce a "grid" of four squares.

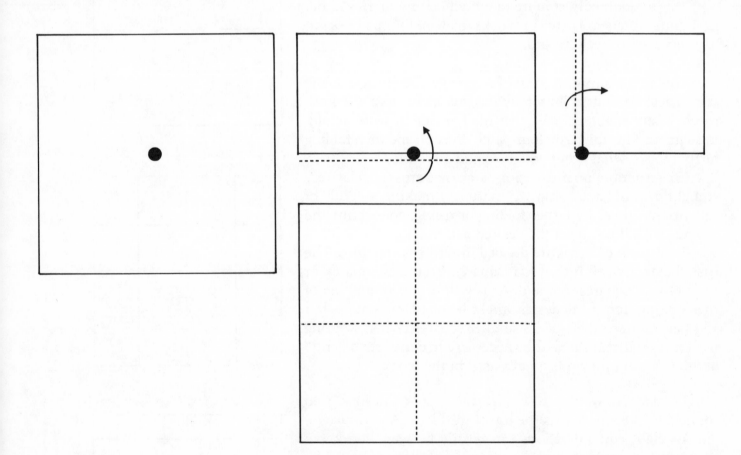

To get 16 squares:

1. Fold the square in half, and then in half again in the same direction.

2. Open the paper and fold it in the other direction in half and then in half again.

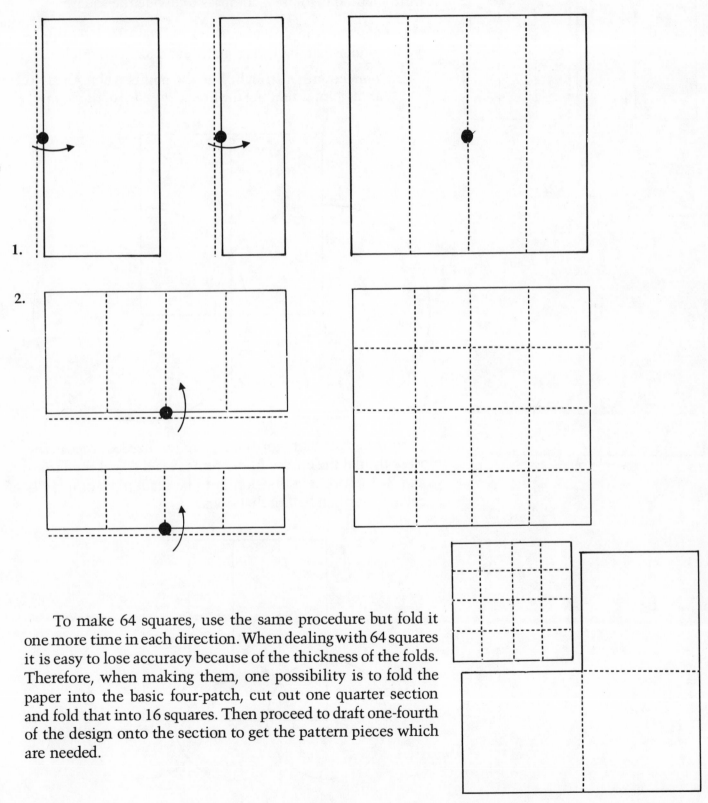

To make 64 squares, use the same procedure but fold it one more time in each direction. When dealing with 64 squares it is easy to lose accuracy because of the thickness of the folds. Therefore, when making them, one possibility is to fold the paper into the basic four-patch, cut out one quarter section and fold that into 16 squares. Then proceed to draft one-fourth of the design onto the section to get the pattern pieces which are needed.

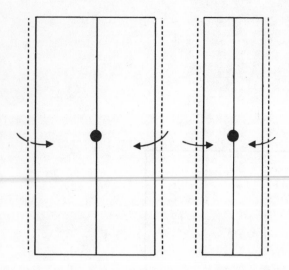

If you want to construct the whole 64 square design on the paper there are three ways to draft it to get the most accuracy. One is to use the method described in Chapter III to make the grid, another is to fold the square into itself from both sides.

A third method is to use a compass to divide the square.

1. Place the compass point on two corners (A and B), open it wider than half the square and make two circles.

2. Connect with a straight line the points where the two circles join, extending the line to the edge of the square.

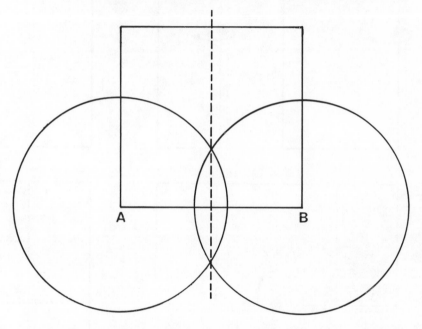

If further divisions of the square are needed, repeat the process by making circles from points A and C and then from C and B. Each time a division is to be made the compass is opened wider than half of that division.

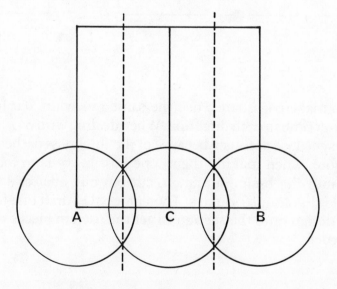

Once a design is classified into its proper category the next question is how many pattern pieces are needed? Once that is answered it is not always necessary to draw the entire design on the paper. For example in *Yankee Puzzle* only one template is needed—a triangle. Divide a square into a four-patch. Working with one quarter section, draw diagonal lines from corner to corner in both directions. These lines will form the triangle needed for the pattern.

It is important to remember that you do not always *see* the basic "grid" divisions within a design. Many times whole areas are colored in, crossing over the division lines of a block as in the diagram below. **Understanding the categories that designs fall into requires your being able to *see through* whole areas and recognize the basic grid underneath.**

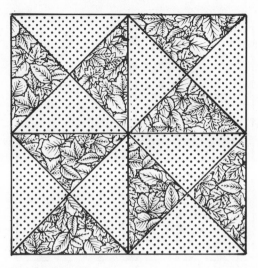

YANKEE PUZZLE

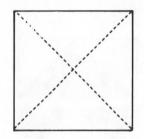

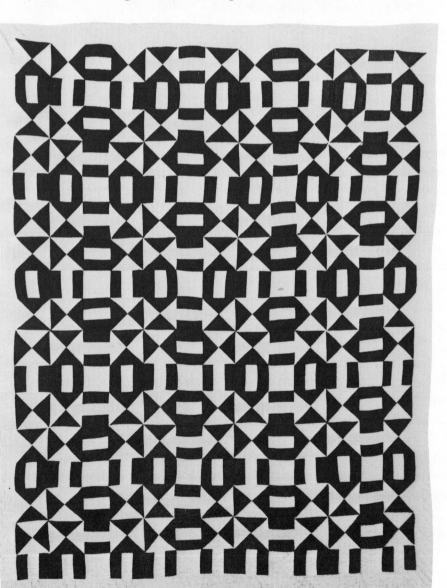

Yankee Puzzle. Blocks have been set together with strips of rectangles and squares to form the overall design, circa 1900. From the collection of Mary Ann Shindle.

17

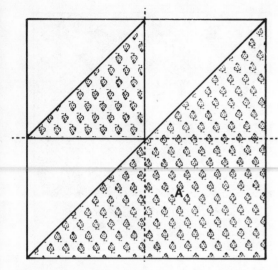

BIRDS IN THE AIR

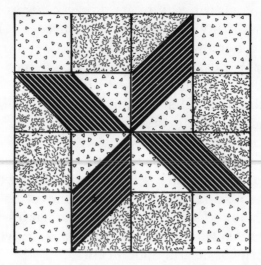

CLAY'S CHOICE   SHOOTING STAR

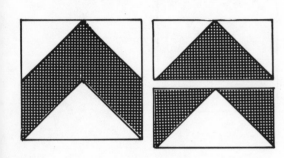

When sewing these types of designs make *one* piece out of the larger units instead of putting them together with two or more smaller pieces. For example with *Birds in the Air* one large triangle, "A," would be cut as opposed to a square and two smaller triangles. With *Clay's Choice* the parallelogram is usually constructed as one piece instead of two separate triangles. The exception is where a piece would have to be "clipped" in order for it to fit. In the case of the design to the left, the dark area would not be made with all one piece but would be broken down into units and pieced with straight lines. Wherever possible try to piece in units where all the seams can be straight lines. This will aid in getting the points to meet.

Category I Four Squares

There are relatively few designs in this category because there is only so much that can be done with four squares. Soon the need comes to break the squares down with further lines as in categories two and three.

Four square patterns are constructed by folding the paper into the basic four-patch (page 14) and then connecting the folds with diagonal lines. This can be done by either folding or drawing lines from corner to corner with a ruler.

A *square within a square* design can be made by folding a four-patch and then folding the center point "A" up to meet corner edges "B."

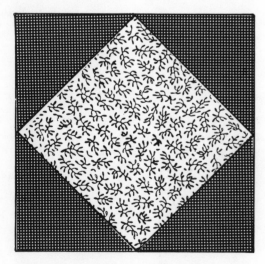

SQUARE WITHIN A SQUARE

This can also be drafted by taking the basic four-patch and connecting points "C" with straight lines.

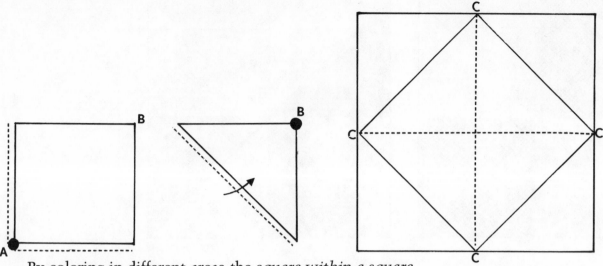

By coloring in different areas the *square within a square* can be changed as follows:

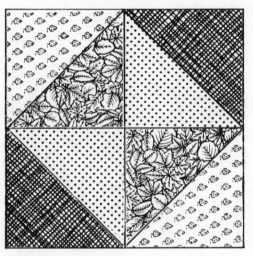

BROKEN DISHES

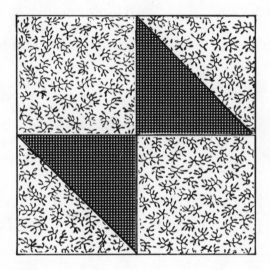

Other four square patterns can be made by connecting the *corners* with diagonal lines either by folding or ruling.

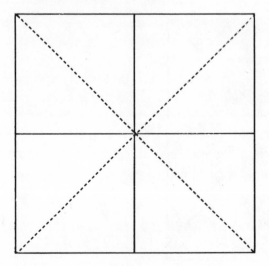

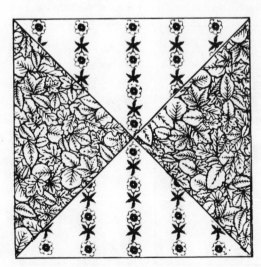

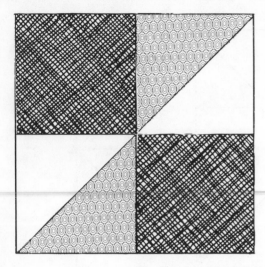

And still others are a combination of a *square within within a square* and diagonal lines from corner to corner. All that is necessary is to color in the appropriate spaces for each design.

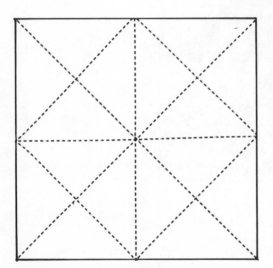

RIGHT AND LEFT

BIG DIPPER OR YANKEE PUZZLE

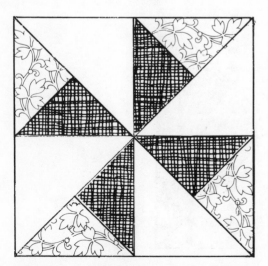

WINDMILL WHIRLIGIG OR TURNSTILE

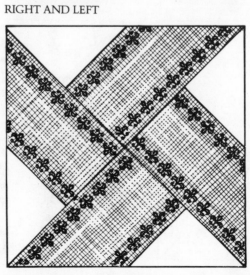

TWIN SISTERS WHIRLWIND OR WATER WHEEL

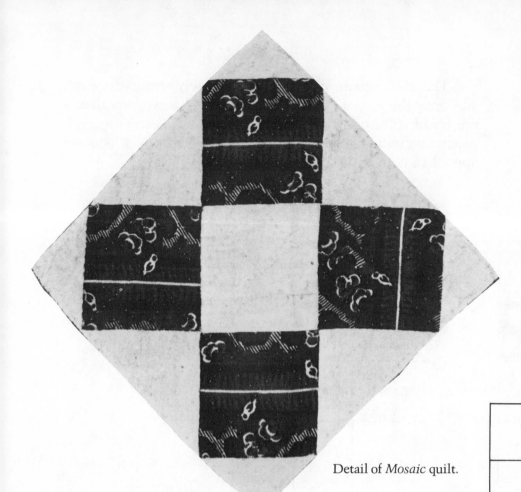

Detail of *Mosaic* quilt.

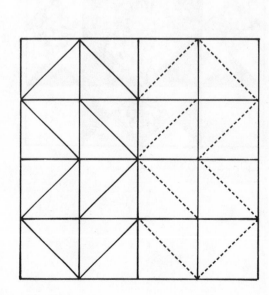

Category II Sixteen Squares

The following 16 square four-patch design can easily be constructed by folding a 16 square "grid" and then connecting the squares according to the layout of the design as in the example below.

STAR PUZZLE

These 16 square patterns are relatively straightforward, and once the proper "grid" for a design is known it is then a matter of coloring in the squares as would be done on graph paper. Just remember that some lines will "cross over" squares and all 16 divisions will not always be seen.

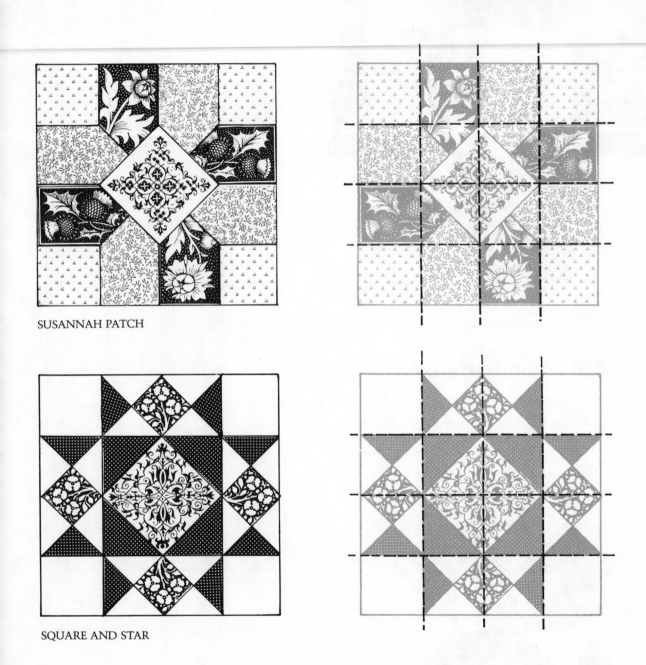

SUSANNAH PATCH

SQUARE AND STAR

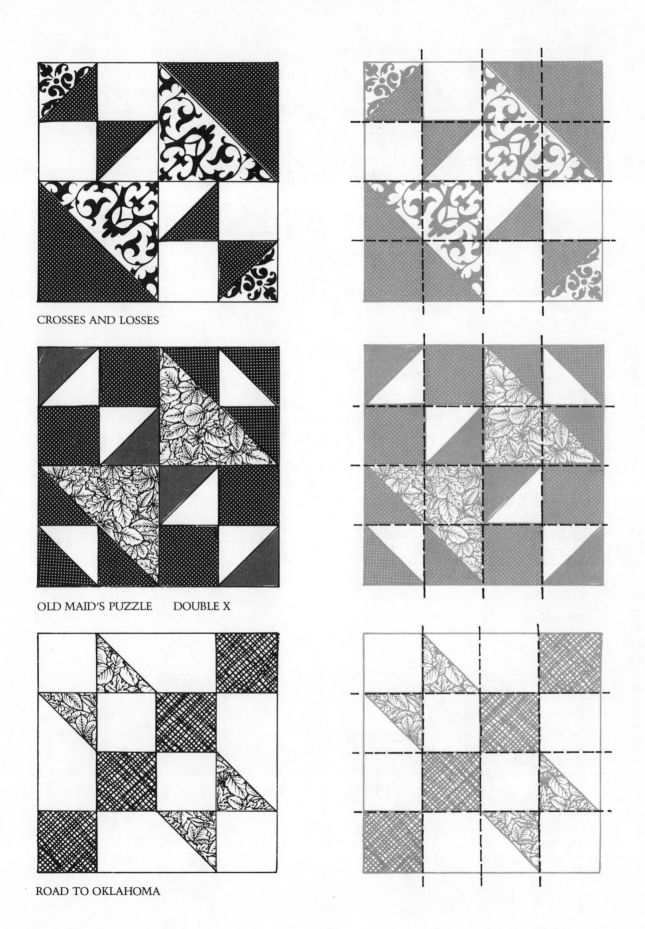

CROSSES AND LOSSES

OLD MAID'S PUZZLE   DOUBLE X

ROAD TO OKLAHOMA

23

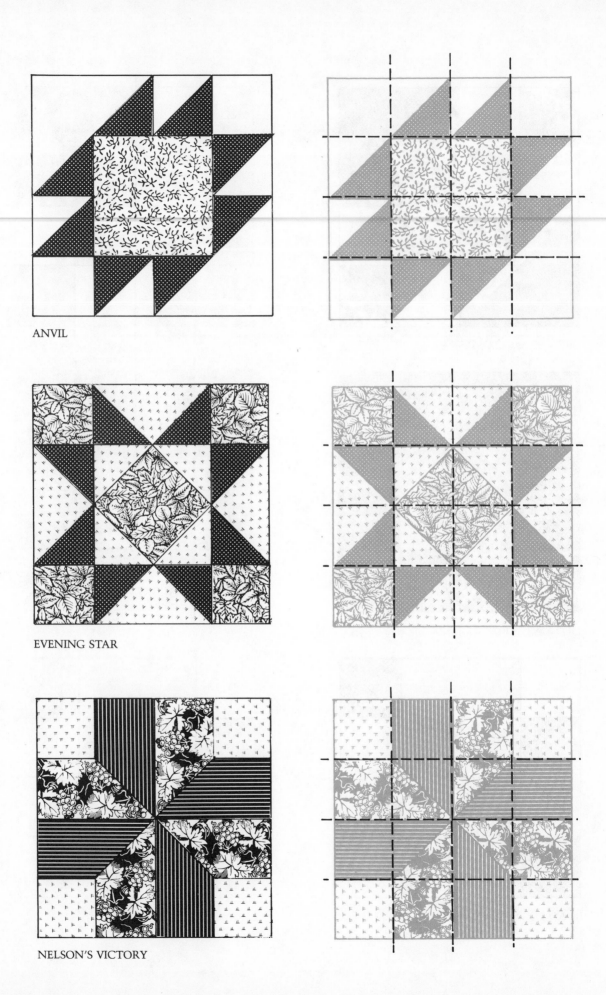

ANVIL

EVENING STAR

NELSON'S VICTORY

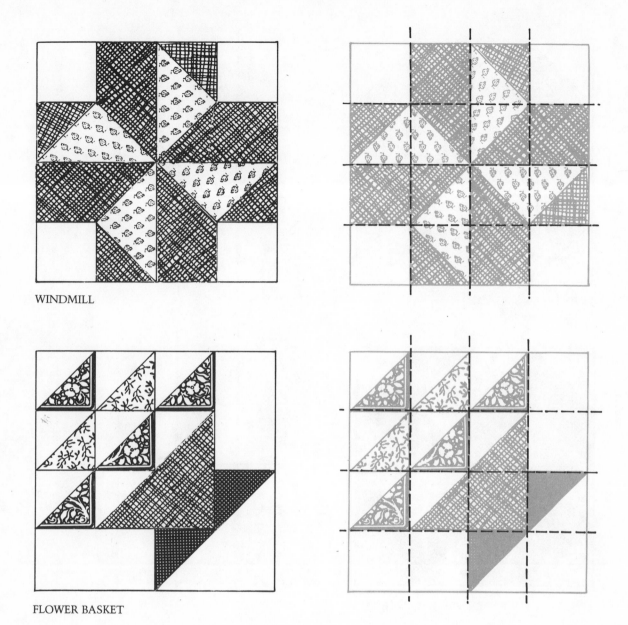

WINDMILL

FLOWER BASKET

The next 16 square four-patch designs are at first glance confusing, but when the grid lines are drawn you can see at once how they are constructed and they are just as easy to draft as the preceding group of patterns. It is interesting to note that the first two designs—*Dutchman's Puzzle* and *Swastika* are exactly the same pattern. The difference in the design comes with color placement.

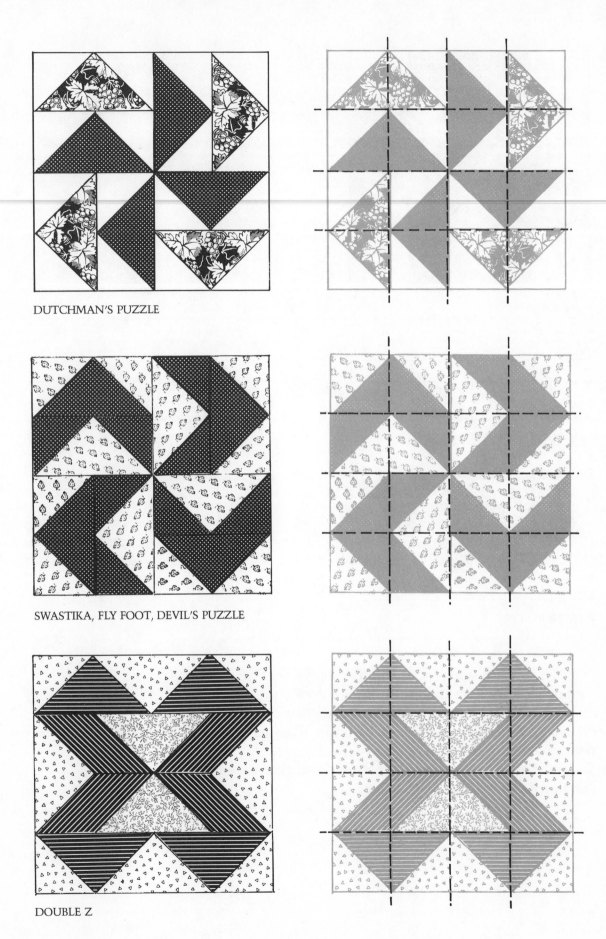

DUTCHMAN'S PUZZLE

SWASTIKA, FLY FOOT, DEVIL'S PUZZLE

DOUBLE Z

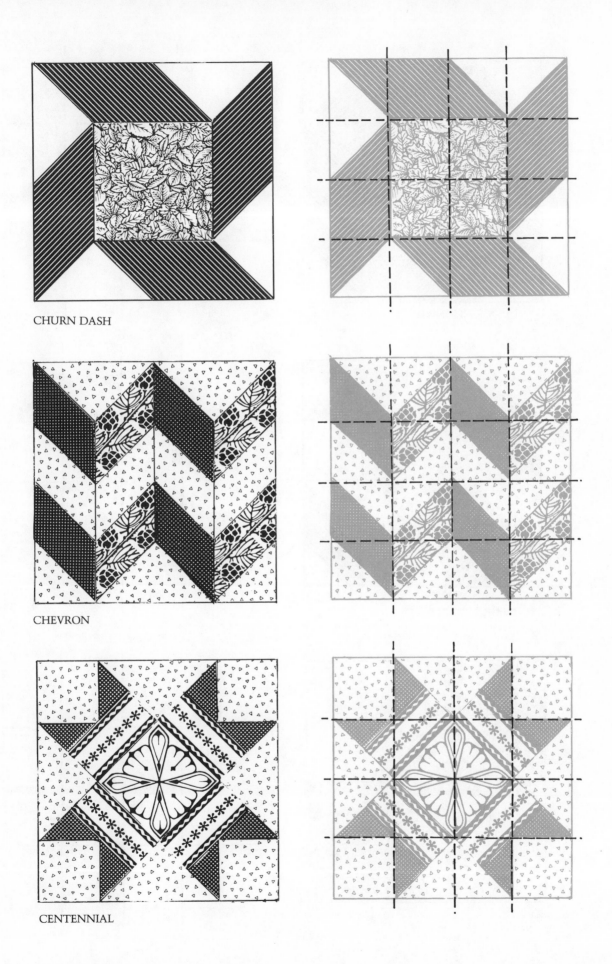

CHURN DASH

CHEVRON

CENTENNIAL

27

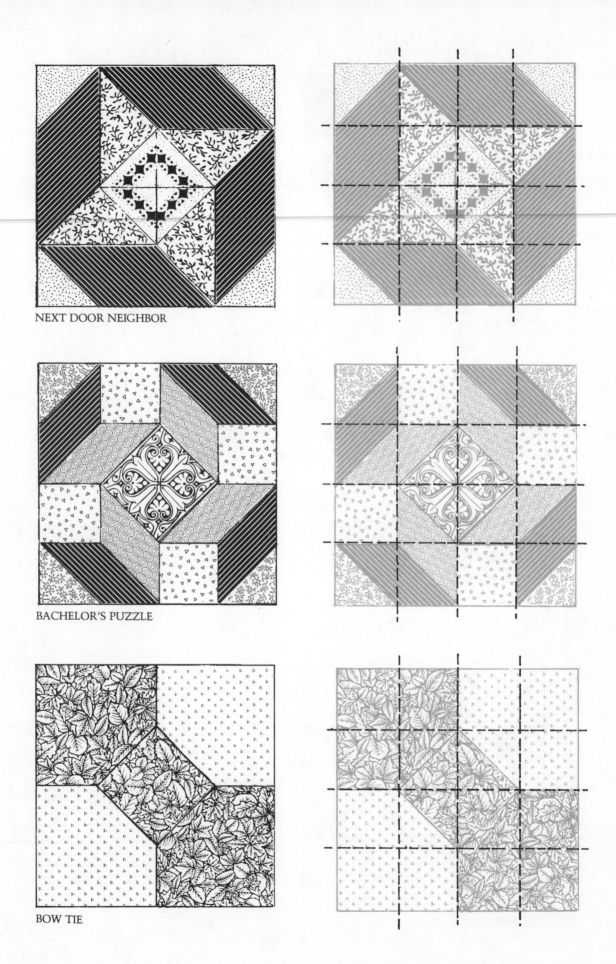

NEXT DOOR NEIGHBOR

BACHELOR'S PUZZLE

BOW TIE

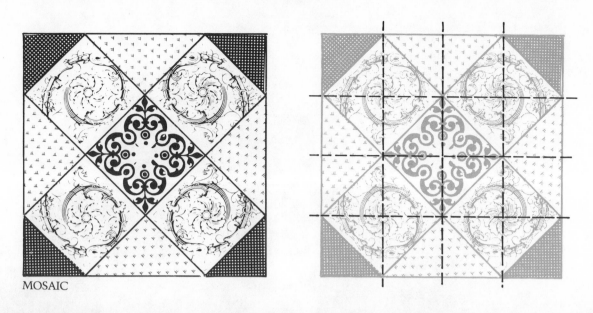

MOSAIC

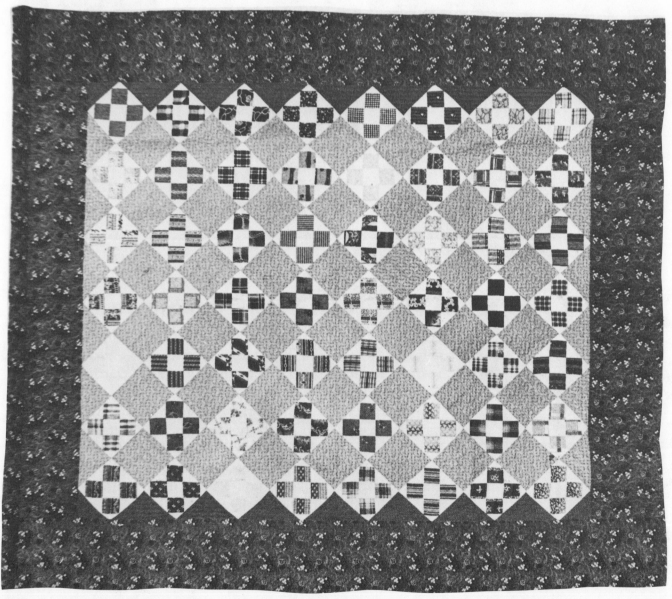

Mosaic. Quilt based on the four-patch, circa 1860. Author's collection.

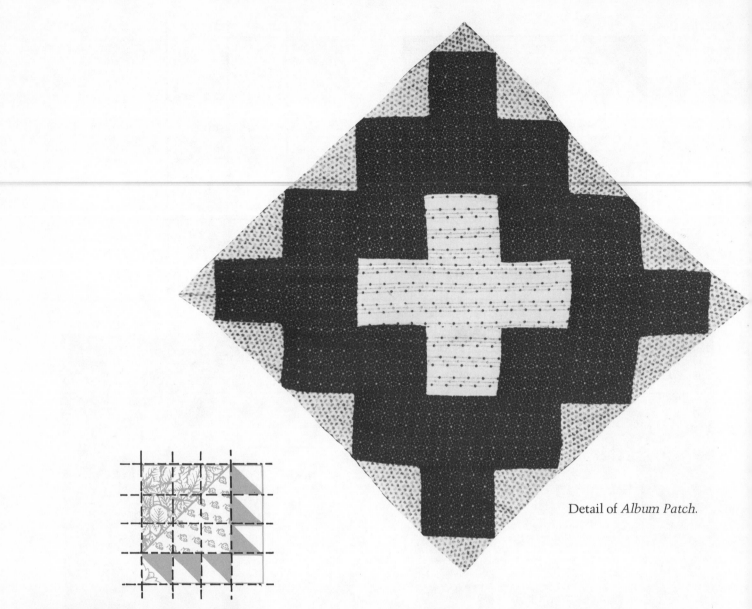

Detail of *Album Patch.*

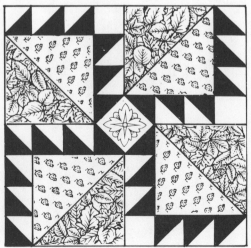

INDIAN TRAIL

Category III Sixty-Four Squares

With 64 square four-patch designs all 64 squares will not necessarily be used individually to construct the patterns. But in order to be able to draft certain elements of the design, the 64 square grid needs to be drafted on the paper.

At first glance some of these designs can be overwhelming. The secret is to break them down into units instead of trying to visualize the layout of the overall patterns. Look at *Indian Trail.* It is a little confusing until you look at only one quarter section of the design. The quarter section has a 16 square grid on it and the design is made by ruling across the grid lines.

As in the designs of the previous categories, once a grid is imposed on the 64 square patterns, it is easy to see how to construct them.

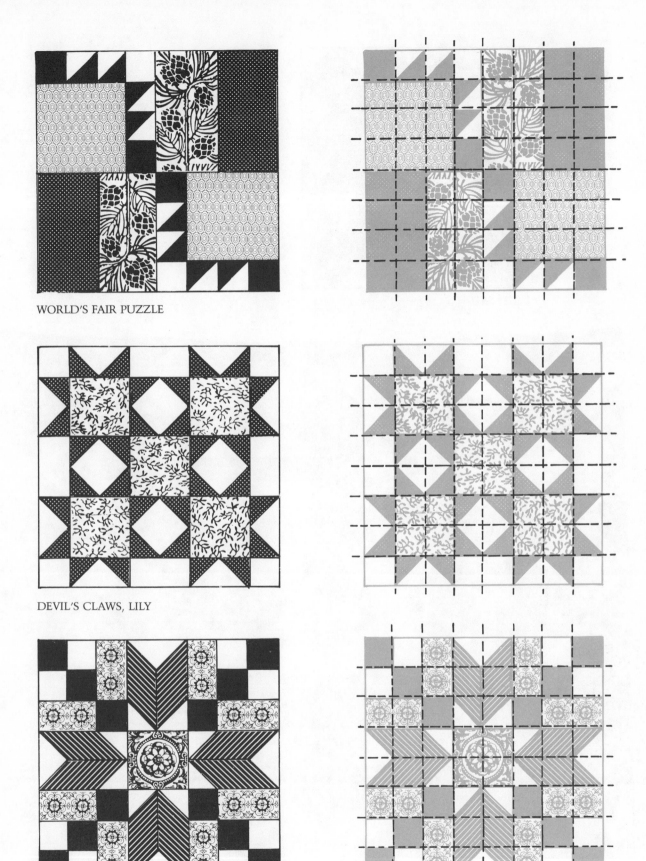

WORLD'S FAIR PUZZLE

DEVIL'S CLAWS, LILY

BLACK BEAUTY

31

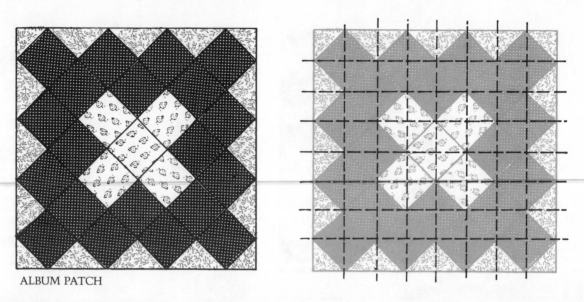

ALBUM PATCH

Album Patch. Quilt top based on the four-patch, circa 1900. Author's collection.

CRAZY ANN

CROSS WITHIN A CROSS

RISING STAR STAR AND SQUARE

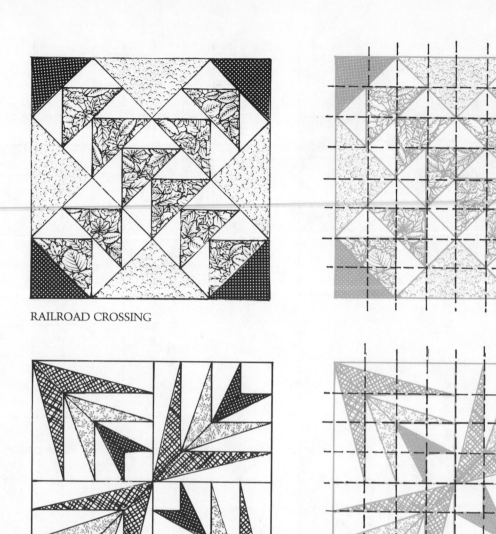

RAILROAD CROSSING

PALM LEAF, HOSANNA

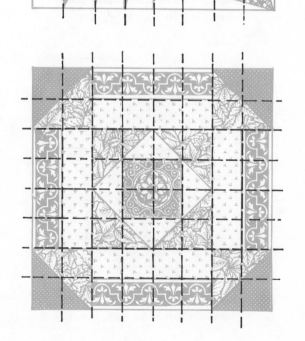

TRIANGLES AND STRIPES

DOUBLE SQUARES

Detail of *Ocean Waves*.

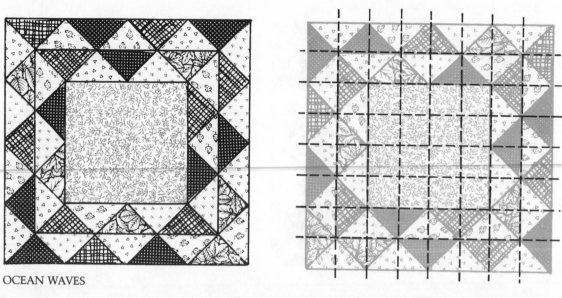

OCEAN WAVES

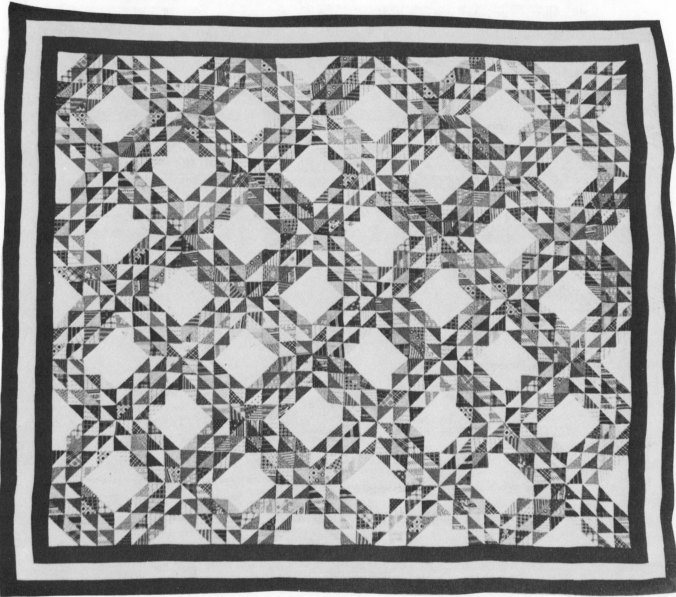

Ocean Waves. This version, circa 1875, shows the units diagonally set. From the collection of Mary Ann Shindle.

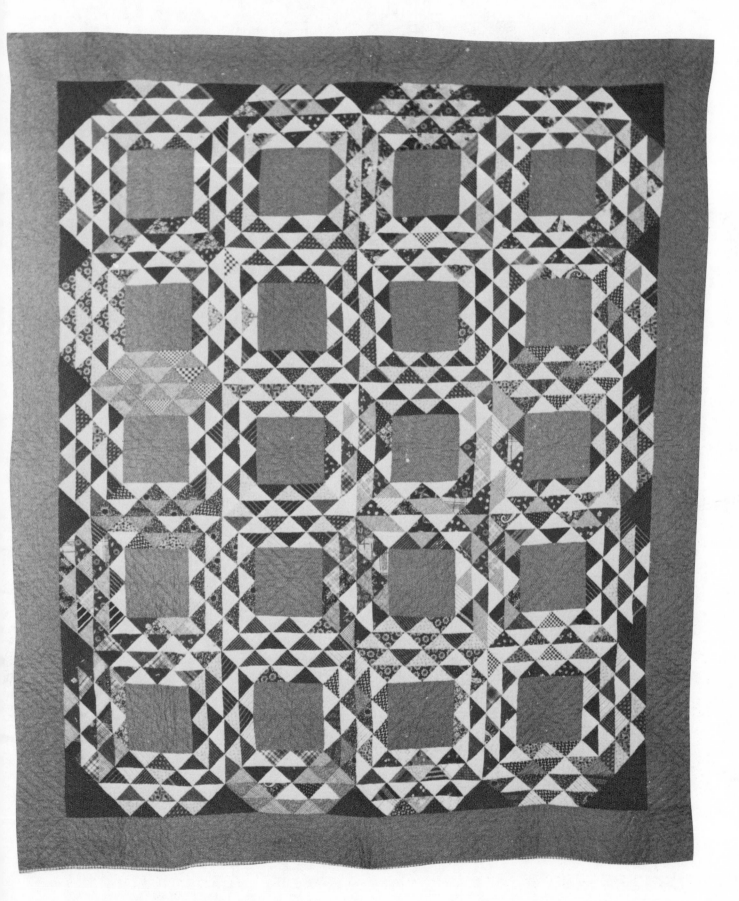

Ocean Waves. This version, circa 1900, shows the blocks set "square."   From the collection of Dick and Ellen Swanson.

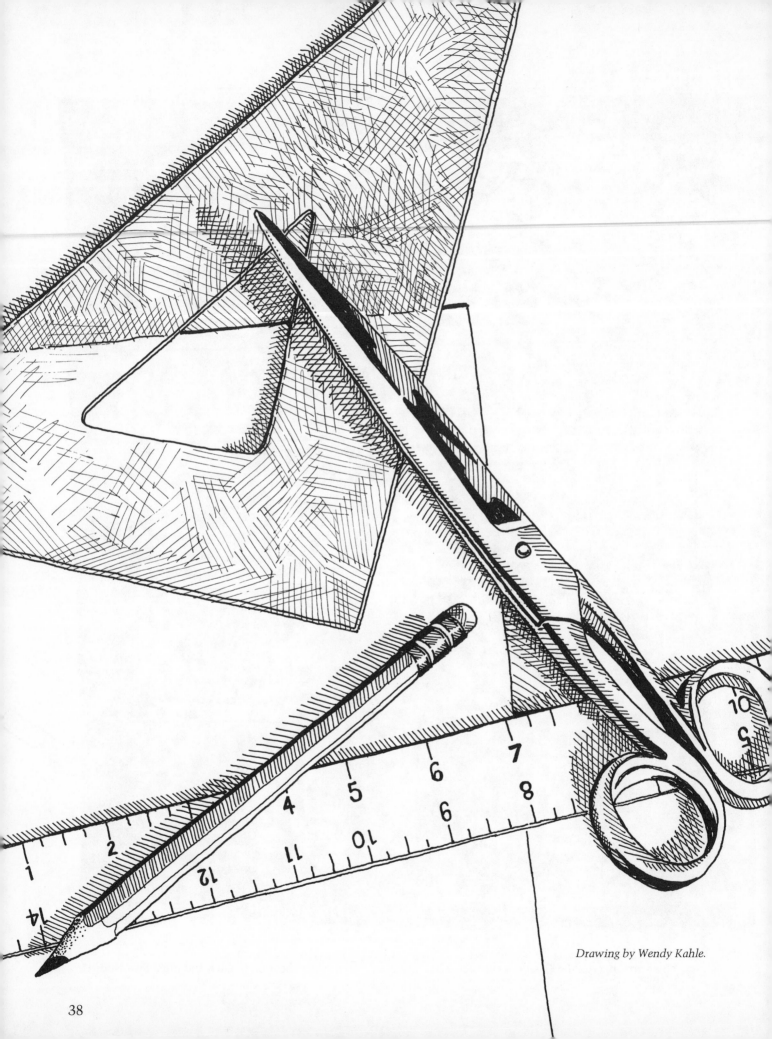

Drawing by Wendy Kahle.

38

CHAPTER III

Dividing an Area into Equal Units

Four-patch "grids," made by repeatedly folding the paper in half, are easy to construct. But when trying to make a grid with nine squares as in nine-patch designs, 25 squares as in a five-patch, 49 squares as in a seven-patch, or when the four-patch has to be divided into 64 smaller squares, it is more difficult to fold the paper accurately. Fold methods for the nine-patch and five-patch are explained in the appropriate chapters. I feel that folding, when done carefully, can be as accurate as the method described here. The advantages of this method are that it is foolproof and it is an excellent way to divide the paper into *any number* of equal divisions.

This simple technique was explained to me by a gentleman who sat next to me on an airplane. Evidently one normally does not learn the concept except in such courses as mechanical drawing, trigonometry or engineering. Don't be put off. You do not need to have a knowledge of these courses to understand the method.

Any size square, rectangle or line can be divided into any number of equal units. All that is needed is a ruler *longer* than the area to be divided, and a triangle.

Basically what needs to be done is to:

1. Mark off on the ruler however many equal divisions are needed for the design (the sum of the inches in the divisions must be *greater* than the width of the area to be divided).

2. Angle the ruler from one corner of the paper square until the end of the last division hits the opposite side.

3. Make a dot on the paper by each of the divisions.

4. Using a triangle make the division lines.

5. Turn the paper and repeat the process to get the division lines in both directions.

To divide a five inch block into thirds, mark off three equal divisions on the ruler.

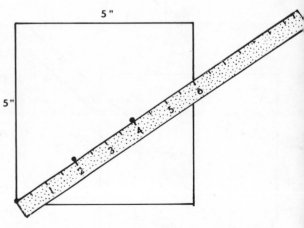

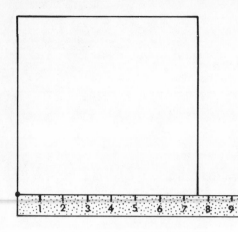

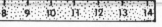

For clarification, I will present some examples using an odd-sized square that cannot easily be divided mathematically or on graph paper. Let's say a 7½" square is needed for a project and that you want to draft a design from the nine-patch category. Therefore the square must be divided into thirds in both directions in order to get a nine-square "grid."

1. Make a 7½ inch square.

2. Find the next number on the ruler greater than 7½ that can be divided evenly by three. In this case it would be nine.

3. Lay the ruler along the bottom edge of the square so that "0" is at the lower left corner.

4. Holding the lower end of the ruler so it does not slip, swing the other end up until number nine hits the right-hand edge of the square.

5. Since 9÷3=3, put a mark every three inches at numbers three and six on the ruler.

6. With a triangle, draw the lines to make the three divisions. By putting the bottom edge of the triangle exactly even with the bottom edge of the paper, it is possible to get perfectly straight divisions the length of the square.

7. Turn the paper and repeat the process.

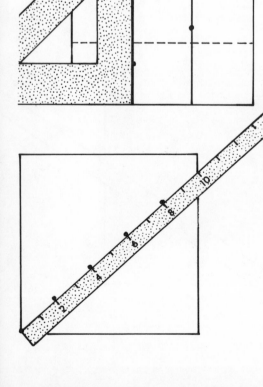

If you want to divide the same 7½" square into fifths for a five-patch pattern, follow the same procedure, but this time a number larger than 7½ has to be found that can be divided evenly by five. Ten is easiest to work with.

Again place the lower end of the ruler on the lower left corner of the square and swing it up until number 10 reaches the right-hand edge of the paper. Now since 10÷5=2, make a mark every two inches, and draw the lines the same as before.

If you next want to divide the square into sevenths for a seven-patch pattern, the procedure will have to be changed. The next number greater than 7½ that would be evenly divisible by seven would be 14. However, when the lower edge of the ruler is placed on the corner of the paper and the other end brought up, you find that 14 is off the edge of the paper.

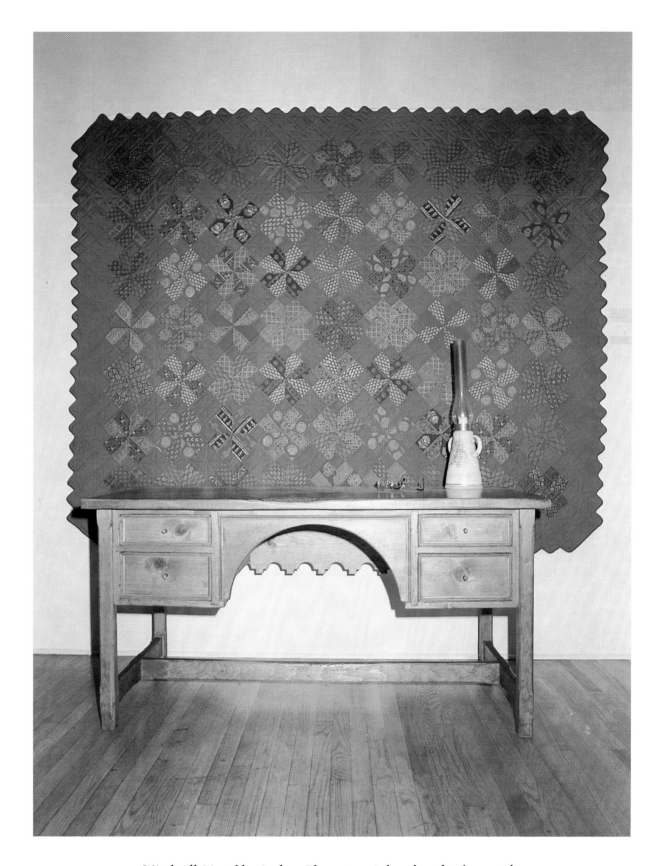

Windmill. Pieced by Author. The pattern is based on the four-patch.
Photograph by Timothy Janaitis.

Lone Star quilt top, circa 1920. This variation of the eight-pointed star
is made by breaking each diamond of the star into smaller diamonds.
A second star has been pieced into the corner squares and triangles.

Photograph by Steve Thompson.

Depending on the size of the block and the number of divisions, this may happen with many of the areas you wish to divide. When the problem occurs one of three things can be done:

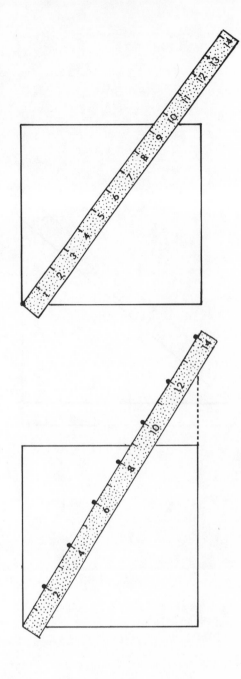

1. Turn the ruler over and use the metric side. Centimeters are smaller units than inches. Therefore, 21 centimeters is longer than 7½ but not so long that it will go off the edge of the paper, and it is evenly divisible by seven. Place the ruler on the paper and pivot it up until 21 centimeters reaches the right-hand edge as before. Now mark off every three centimeters to divide the square into sevenths.

2. If you don't want to use centimeters or don't have a metric ruler, then go to half inches. Seven will go into 10½, 1½ times. Therefore, pivot the ruler until 10½ reaches the edge of the block and mark off every 1½ inches.

3. The third solution to the problem is to extend the right-hand edge of the square with a line. Use 14 inches on the ruler, which can be divided evenly by seven and pivot the ruler until 14 hits the line extension.

4. Then, as before, make a mark every two inches. Even though some of the division marks will be off the square, by using a large triangle you can still make perfectly even lines.

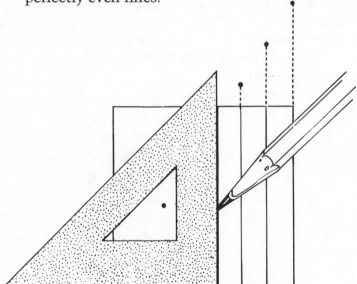

I have demonstrated this method of division on a 7½″ square, but it can be used on *any* size square, rectangle or line. For example, to divide a 19″ line into nine equal units (perhaps for the border of a quilt), draw the line, place a triangle on the line with the right-angle edge resting on one end of it and draw another line perpendicular to it. Twenty-seven is the next number greater than 19 that can be evenly divided by nine, so take a yardstick and proceed as before. Pivot the yardstick until 27 inches hits the perpendicular line, mark off every three inches and use a triangle to draw the division lines.

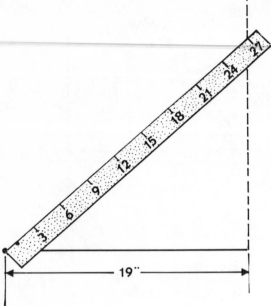

This method of dividing a line is also useful for proportionately enlarging or decreasing rectangles. When planning the size of a rectangular quilt or when drafting rectangular patterns (discussed in Chapter XII), quilters will find this method to be particularly helpful.

If you like the proportions of a 5 x 7 inch design but want to make it larger so that it is 12 inches high, yet proportionately the same, it is necessary to find the width of the rectangle.

1. Draw a 5 x 7 inch rectangle on a piece of paper and draw a line from the lower left corner through the upper right corner, extending the line beyond the rectangle.

2. Mark 12" on the triangle and, placing it on the paper so the lower edge touches the bottom of the rectangle, move it along the bottom until the 12" mark touches the diagonal line.

3. Draw a 12 inch line along the perpendicular edge of the triangle. That will give the right-hand edge of the new rectangle. To close off the top, mark 12 inches along the left edge of the rectangle and draw a line across the top.

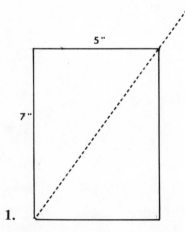

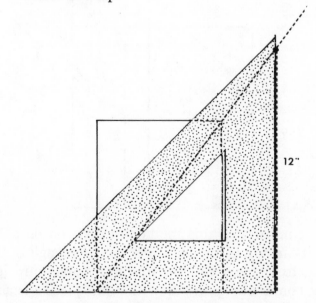

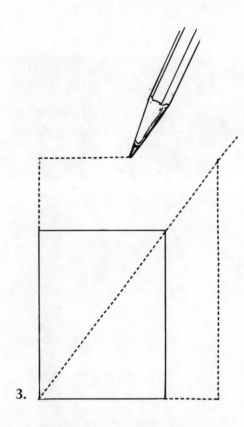

3.

You will find that when you proportionately increase a 5 x 7 inch rectangle so that one side is 12 inches, the other side will be $8\frac{5}{7}$ inches. Any size rectangle can be enlarged in this manner. The diagram below shows a few examples. If you want to use this process in planning a quilt, have one inch represent one foot.

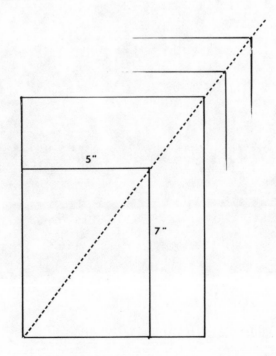

5"

7"

Nine-Patch. ''Diagonally-set'' nine-patch quilt, circa 1910. Author's collection.

CHAPTER **IV**

Nine-Patch

There are perhaps more nine-patch quilts in existence today than those of any other pattern. Sewing a basic nine-patch block, composed of nine squares—five darks and four lights or vice versa—marked the start of many a young girl's quilting experience. This design was usually made into a "scrap" quilt composed of leftover bits and pieces of cloth. Even though it is nothing more than squares sewn together, the design has a simple elegance and can look very different each way it is used.

The nine-patch is one of the largest categories of quilt designs and numerous patterns have been created by further divisions of the basic nine units. Most of these can be put into one of two categories. The first is the basic nine square grid where three equal divisions are seen across the block, and the second is that same grid with each section divided in half. This produces a 36 square grid—or six equal divisions across the block.

To make the basic nine square "grid" either use the method discussed in Chapter III or the fold method described below:

1. Cut a square of paper the size of the "finished" block.

2. Fold one end into thirds, working with the three sections to make sure they are absolutely equal along that edge. Pinch the folds only at the edge. Turn to the opposite end and repeat the process.

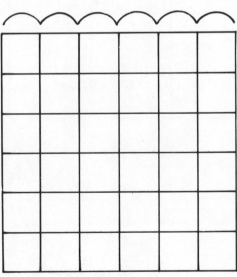

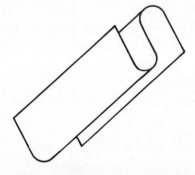
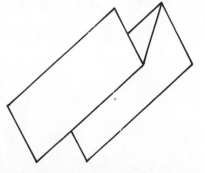

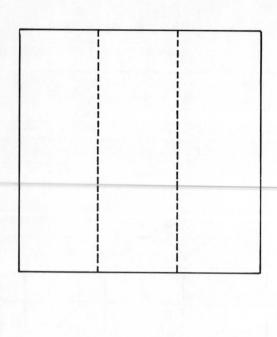

3. Take hold of both ends of the paper where they have been creased and make the folds the length of the block.

4. Open the paper, turn it around and repeat the process.

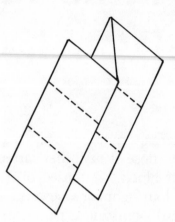

5. When finished, the paper will be divided into nine equal squares.

6. For a 36 square grid, fold the paper one more time in each direction before it is opened.

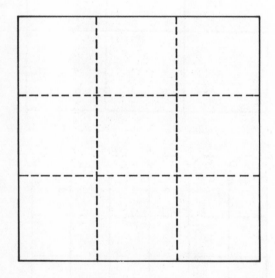

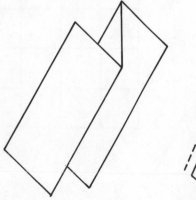

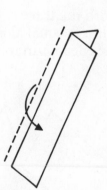

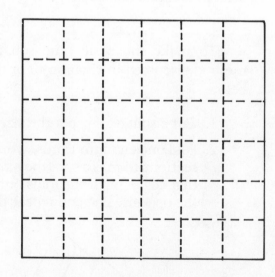

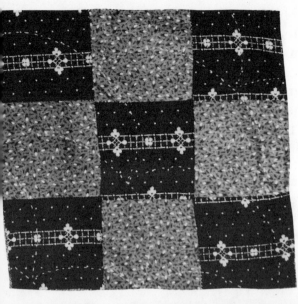

Nine-Patch block. Detail.

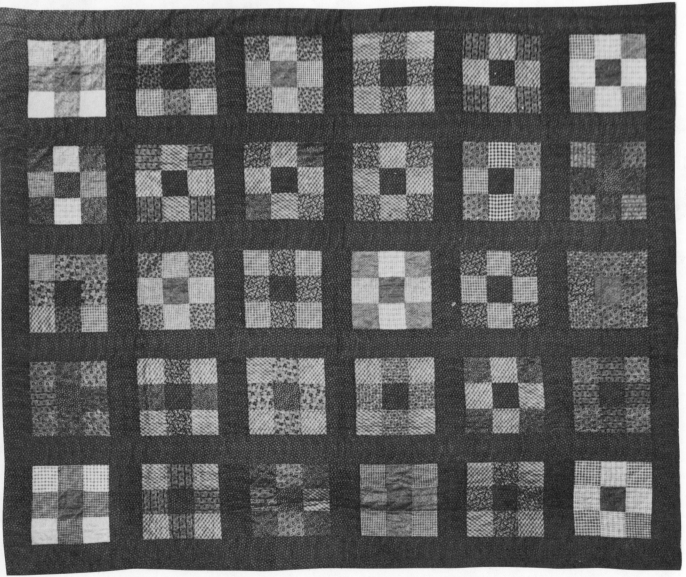

Nine-Patch. "Square-set" basic nine-patch quilt, circa 1910. Author's collection.

ROLLING STONE

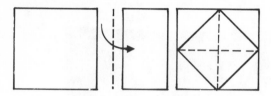

With many nine-patch patterns once the basic "grid" has been made, it is not necessary to draft the whole design on the paper. Find out how many pattern pieces are needed, cut out one or more of the squares from the basic nine-patch and fold them to get the templates. Treat the individual squares as separate units. Sometimes they will be folded into another nine-patch, other times into a four-patch. The following examples will illustrate this technique.

Three pattern pieces are needed for *Rolling Stone*—a rectangle, a square and a small triangle. Cut out two of the basic squares of the nine-patch. For the rectangle, fold one square in half lengthwise.

To get the square and triangle, take the other square and fold it to make a square within a square as on page 18.

Three templates are needed for *54-40 or Fight*. Cut out two squares. Fold one into a four-patch. Fold the second in half lengthwise. Open the paper and rule from the upper corners down to the center.

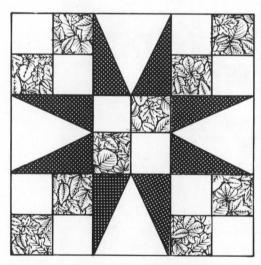

54-40 OR FIGHT

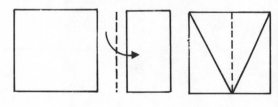

54-40 or Fight.

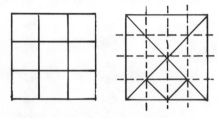

DOLLY MADISON STAR

Dolly Madison Star.

Three templates are needed for *Dolly Madison Star*.
Cut out three squares from the nine-patch grid. One
is the corner square. The second has to be divided
into a small nine-patch. Divide the third square into
a 16 square grid and rule diagonally across the squares
to form the small triangles.

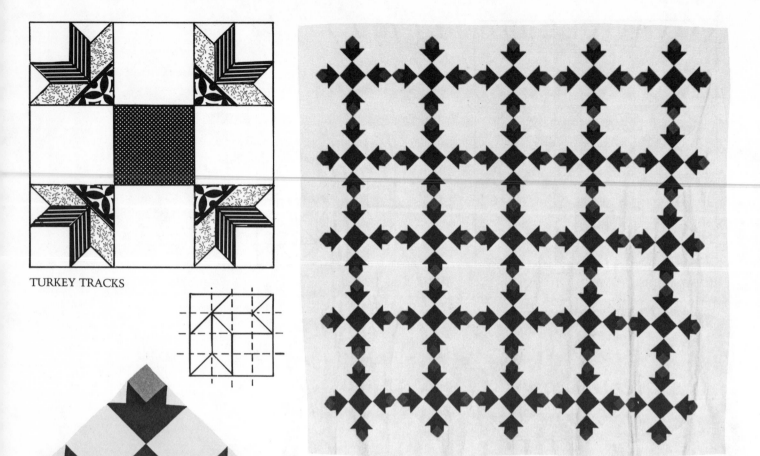

TURKEY TRACKS

Detail of *Turkey Tracks.*

Turkey Tracks. Quilt top. From the collection of Dick and Ellen Swanson.

Five templates are needed for *Turkey Tracks.* Cut out two squares. Nothing needs to be done with the first. Construct a 16 square grid on the second and rule as if it were graph paper to get the design.

Four templates are needed for *Beggar Block.* The center square is one basic square of the original nine-patch. Fold a second square into a small nine-patch and rule across the grid to get the smaller pieces in the design.

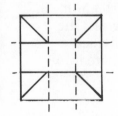

BEGGAR BLOCK

MORNING STAR

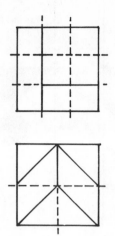

JOSEPH'S COAT

Seven pattern pieces are needed for *Morning Star.*
Cut out three squares. Divide one into a nine-patch
and rule along the grid to get the pattern pieces
needed for one of the squares. Divide another into
a four-patch and rule to get the pattern pieces for the
other square. The third square remains unchanged.

Six templates are needed for *Joseph's Coat.* Cut out
three squares. One remains the same as the basic
square. One square needs to be divided into a four-
patch and ruled accordingly. Divide the third square
into thirds one direction, in half the other direction
and then rule accordingly.

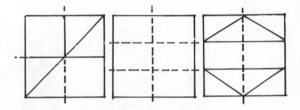

The following designs can all be drafted in the same manner as those above, that is, by cutting out one or more of the
basic squares and making the pattern pieces from them.

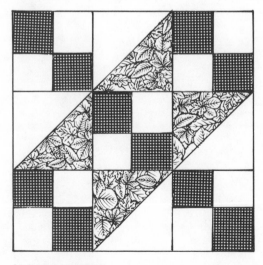

JACOB'S LADDER

SHOO-FLY

WINGED SQUARE

OHIO STAR

LONDON ROADS

SAWTOOTH PATCHWORK

AIR CASTLE

Many nine-patch designs cannot be easily drafted by cutting out individual squares. For certain patterns it is best to construct the grid and draft the entire design on the paper by ruling from the grid lines as in the diagrams below.

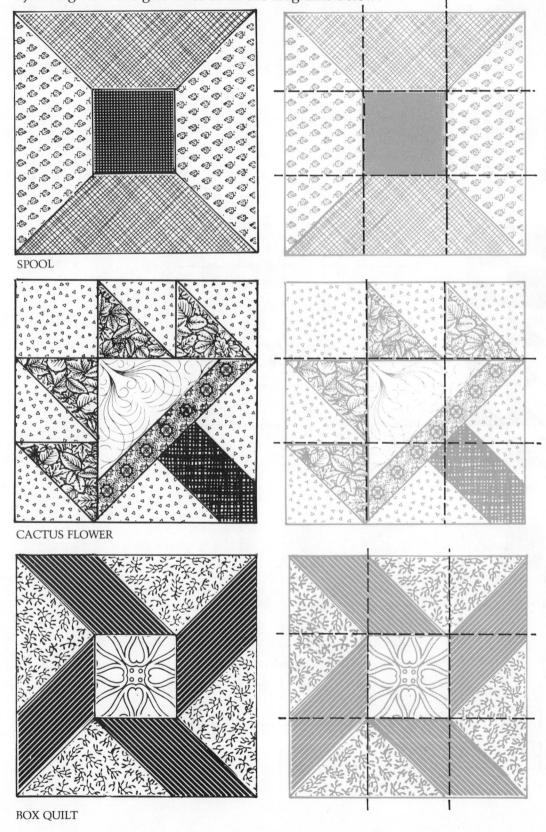

SPOOL

CACTUS FLOWER

BOX QUILT

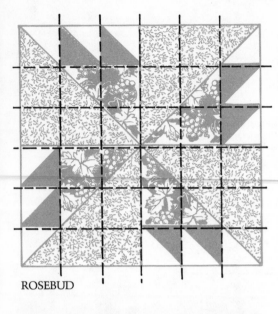

ROSEBUD

Many 36 square nine-patch patterns can be drafted in the same way. These designs are often hard to categorize at first, but when you impose the 36 square grid on the design, it is then easier to see how the block is constructed.

PINE TREE

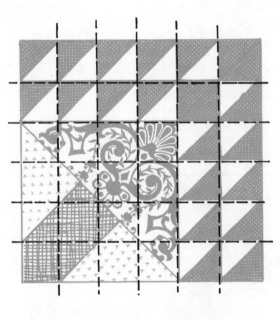

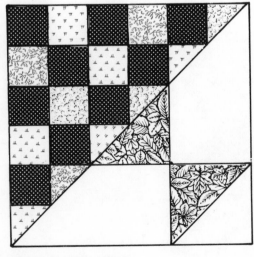

STEPS TO THE ALTAR

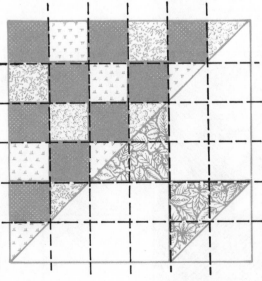

CHERRY BASKET

UNION

ROLLING PIN WHEEL

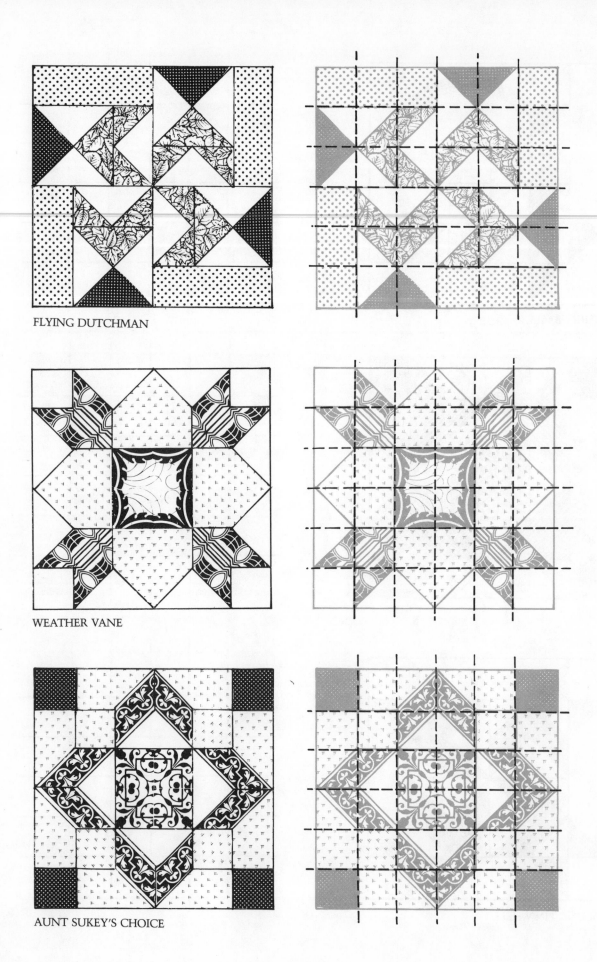

FLYING DUTCHMAN

WEATHER VANE

AUNT SUKEY'S CHOICE

Kaleidoscope. By Author.
Photograph by Steve Thompson.

Castle Wall. By Author. Two versions of the same design. Totally different effects can be achieved depending on the fabrics used.

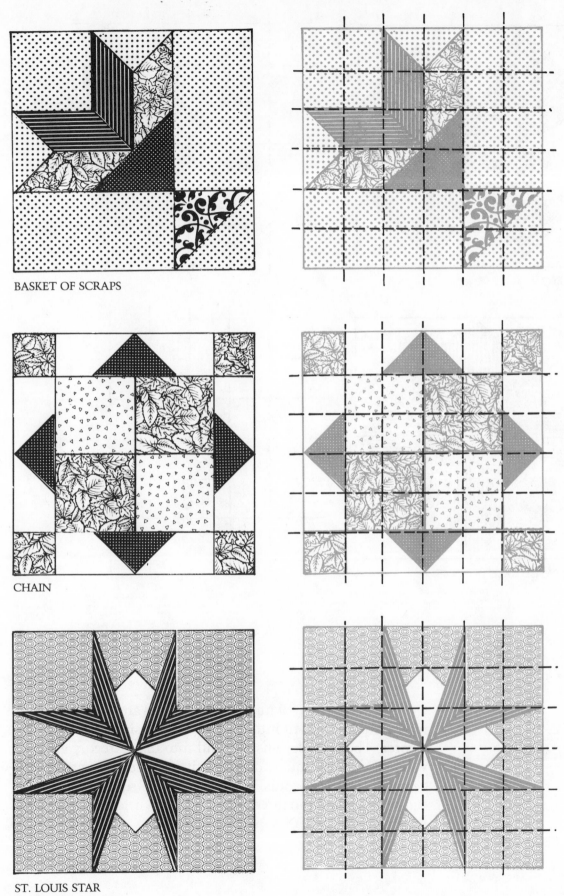

BASKET OF SCRAPS

CHAIN

ST. LOUIS STAR

57

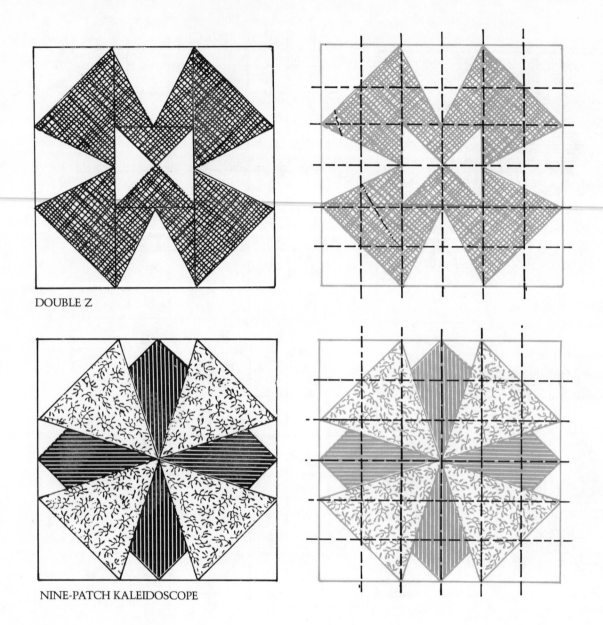

DOUBLE Z

NINE-PATCH KALEIDOSCOPE

The next group of nine-patch patterns are ones which one might think would fit into Chapter VIII, Designs with a Square Center. The only designs that fall into that category are ones where the center square does not fit into the grid of any other category. In other words, it is an "isolated" square. The center square in each of the three patterns shown below is the middle square of the basic nine-patch.

NONSENSE

GENTLEMAN'S FANCY

CAPITAL T

59

With the next three patterns, the diagonally set center square is actually a "square within a square" set into the middle unit of the basic nine-patch. By imposing a 36 square grid on these designs it is easier to see how to draft them.

SKY ROCKET

SWING IN THE CENTER

CATS AND MICE

Mrs. Cleveland's Choice is one of the few nine-patch designs based on a grid not of three or six equal divisions across the block, but 12. Once a 144 square grid is imposed on the design you can see how the pattern is made.

MRS. CLEVELAND'S CHOICE

Mrs. Cleveland's Choice. Wall hanging by Author.

Mexican Star.

Five-Patch

A fter the four- and nine-patch, the five-patch is probably the third largest category of quilt patterns. These are designs where the square is divided into a basic grid of 25 squares, or five equal divisions across the block. Some of these designs are further divided so that the block has a grid of 100 squares or ten divisions across the square.

If you are working with a ten inch block, it is very easy to divide the paper into 25 equal squares—just use your ruler to mark two inch segments in both directions on the paper. One can always divide the size of the square by five to get the divisions, but it is not always possible to work with a convenient sized square. Many patchwork projects require the use of odd-sized blocks. If an eight inch block is needed the paper would have to be divided into five divisions of $1^6/_{10}"$ each. An 11 inch block would have five sections that each measured $2^1/_5"$. These divisions are difficult to make accurately by measuring with a ruler because rulers are usually not divided into tenths.

All the "odd-sized blocks" that one needs for patchwork plus my determination to find a way to fold a piece of paper to get a five-patch led to my discovery of the following method of dividing a square into 25 smaller squares for a five-patch design. The method of dividing a square discussed in Chapter III is, perhaps, easier to remember and an accurate way to divide the paper for a five-patch, but for those who would prefer folding, the method will be described.

I must give credit to several of my students who showed me various ways to fold a square to get a five-pointed star. Without that knowledge I could not have proceeded. However, when I saw that one *could* fold a square to get a five-pointed star, it also seemed logical that there must be some way of folding a square to get five equal divisions across one edge.

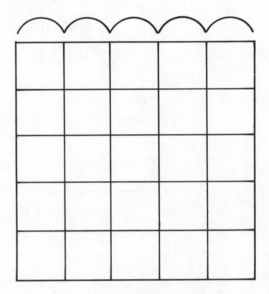

Pine Tree.

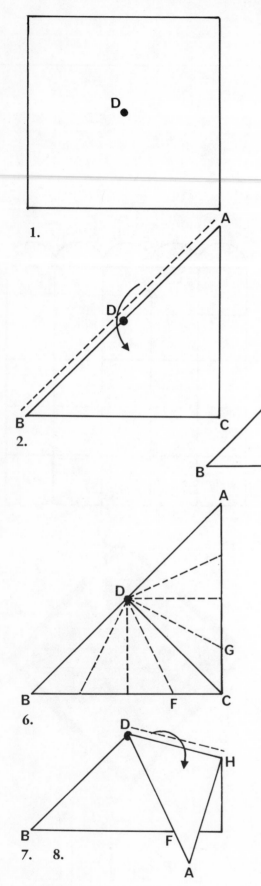

1.

2.

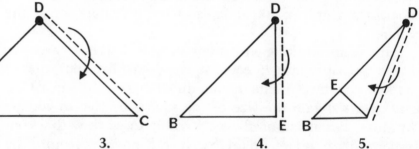

3.

4.

5.

6.

7. 8.

After going through piles of paper squares and working for hours, I finally thought that I had found a way. I was teaching a class in California and I showed them the method that I had discovered. They all tried it and almost in unison everyone said, "It doesn't come out even." I was devastated. I went back to my motel room and spent several more hours working. Finally, I found a correct way to do it.

1. Decide what size block you want and cut a square of paper that size.

2. Fold the paper in half diagonally.

3. Now fold diagonally again (bring A down to B).

4. Next fold line DC over to line DB.

5. Finally, fold line DE over to line DB.

What you have now is a square that has been folded into sixteenths. Always keep in mind where center point "D" is.

6. Open the paper to where it was after the first fold.

   Mark center line DC.

7. Now look for the fold line just to the left of center line DC (line DF) and fold line DA over to meet line DF.

   It is very important that the edge of line DA is touching the entire edge of line DF. You are folding *from* the center of the paper. It is helpful if you put a finger on center point D while folding.

8. Crease and make a pencil mark at point "H."

9. Open the last fold and look for the fold line just to the *right* of the center line DC (Fold DG).

   This time, again *folding from the center point*, fold line DA over to meet line DG.

10. Crease and make another pencil mark at point "I."

64

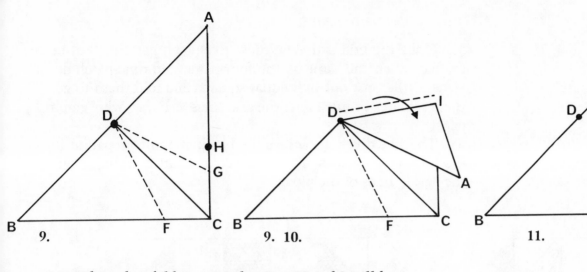

9.

9. 10.

11.

11. When that fold is opened points H and I will be marked along one edge of the paper. You are no longer concerned with any of the folds—only those two marks. They are the *middle* division of the five-patch block.

12. Using a triangle erect lines perpendicular to line AC at points I and H.

13. To get the two divisions either side of the middle one:

    a. Fold point A in to meet point I and crease.

    b. Next fold line BC up to meet line H.

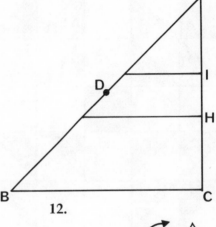

12.

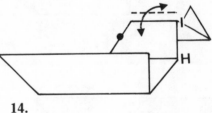

14.

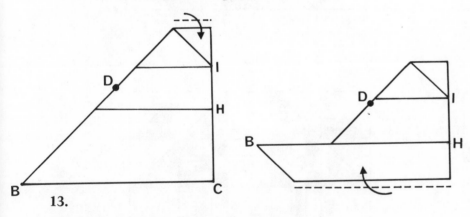

13.

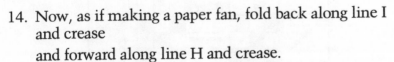

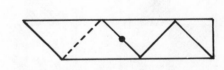

14. Now, as if making a paper fan, fold back along line I and crease

and forward along line H and crease.

This will produce five equal divisions of the block.

15. When the paper is opened the square will look like diagram 15.

Place a ruler along the dotted lines and draw to the edges of the block to form a 25 square grid.

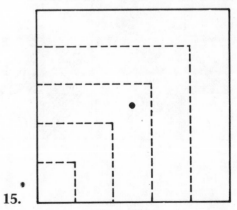

15.

Once the grid is drawn, most five-patch patterns will be drafted much the same as the four-patch and nine-patch designs. Either cut out individual squares and fold them to get the templates or rule along the grid lines as if they were graph paper.

The five divisions across the block are quite apparent in the following designs. They are easy to draft by ruling along the "grid" lines of the block.

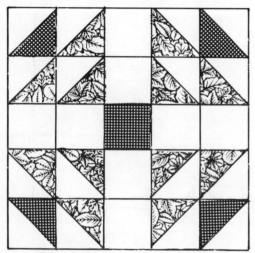

WEDDING RING

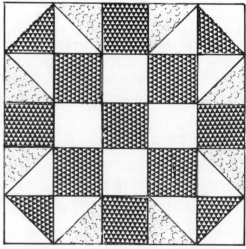

SISTER'S CHOICE

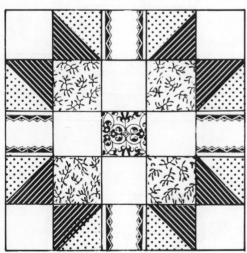

FOUR X STAR

GOOSE IN THE POND
In the case of this pattern one grid square will need to be cut out and folded into a nine-patch.

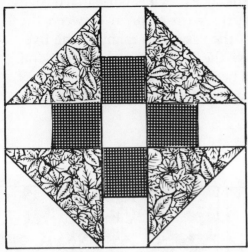

DOUBLE WRENCH

PROVIDENCE QUILT BLOCK

CAKE STAND

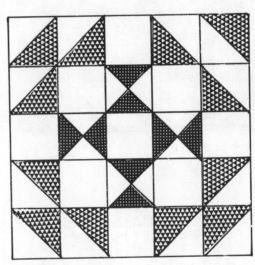

HANDY ANDY

Many five-patch designs are deceptive, just as some nine-patch patterns were, because they appear to belong in the "square in the center" category. Particularly misleading are the five-patch designs that have the square extended to the edges of the block to create "bars".

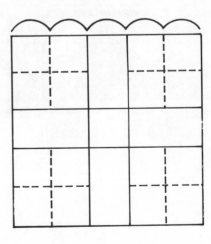

Many of the "bar" patterns appear as if a four-patch design had been separated into fourths with a bar in between the divisions. This is essentially the case with many of the five-patch patterns. Once you have the 25 square grid and mark off the center bars, you will then be working with the four squares in one section as if it were a four-patch to get the templates as in the designs below.

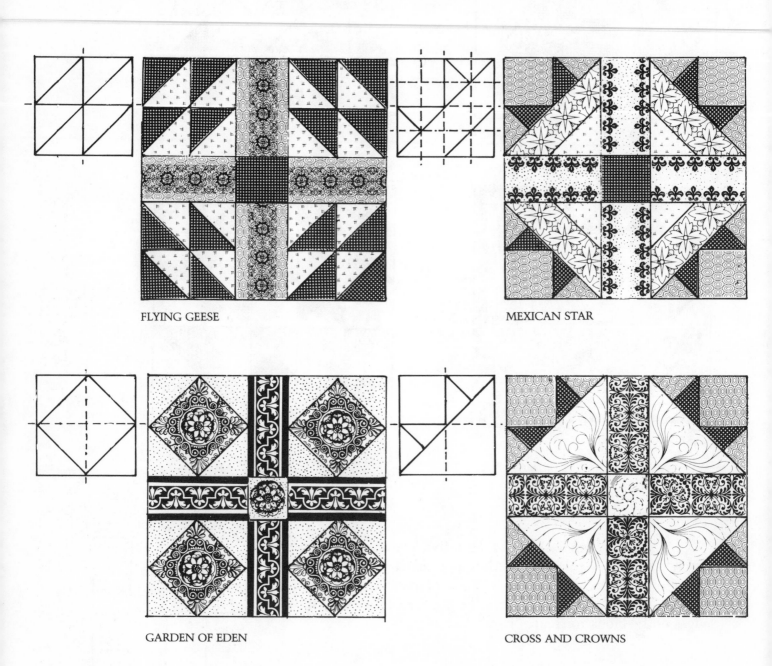

FLYING GEESE

MEXICAN STAR

GARDEN OF EDEN

CROSS AND CROWNS

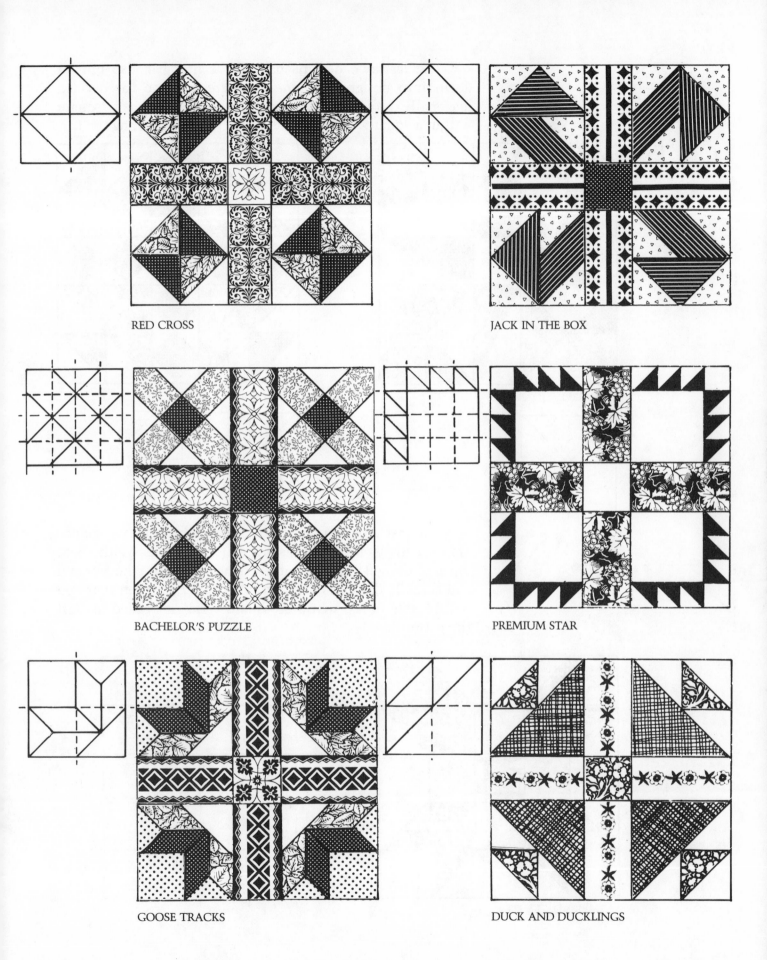

RED CROSS

JACK IN THE BOX

BACHELOR'S PUZZLE

PREMIUM STAR

GOOSE TRACKS

DUCK AND DUCKLINGS

69

The last two designs have the center bar also broken down into designs. *Pinwheel Square* has one bar divided diagonally from corner to corner and *Bird's Nest* has a "square within a square" design done in each square forming the bar.

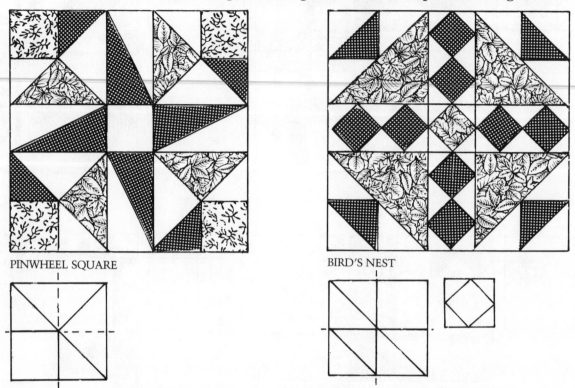

PINWHEEL SQUARE

BIRD'S NEST

The last group of designs are ones which at first glance are difficult to recognize as five-patch patterns. With these types of designs, many times it is necessary to take a pencil and actually draw the division lines. It is only then that you will be able to see that a 25 square "grid" is needed to draft the pattern.

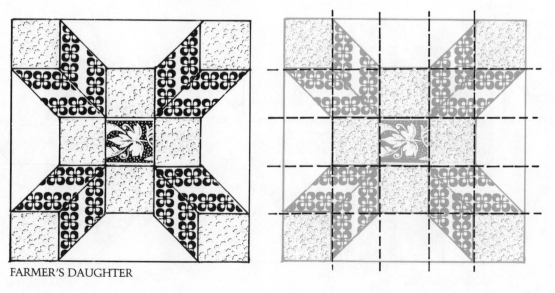

FARMER'S DAUGHTER

QUEEN CHARLOTTE'S CROWN
INDIAN MEADOW

JOSEPH'S COAT

SQUARE AND A HALF

71

ST. LOUIS STAR

GRANDMOTHER'S CROSS

MEMORY BLOCK

Variation on a Star. Made by drafting a large eight-pointed star and
breaking it down into smaller inner squares as in *Star and Chains.*
By Author.
Photograph by Steve Thompson.

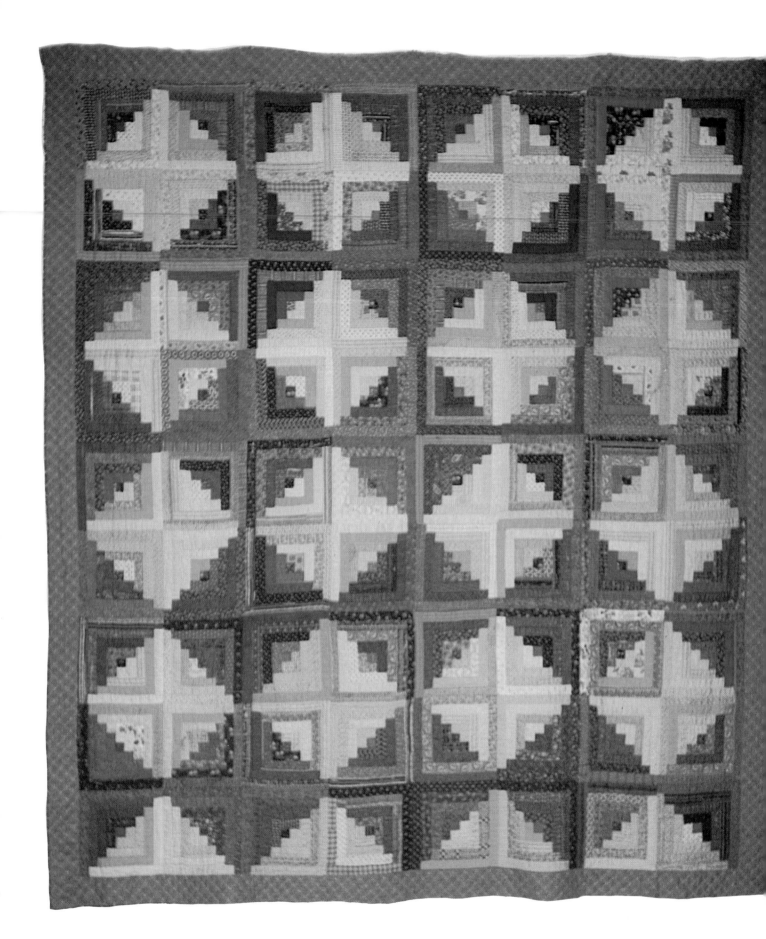

Log Cabin, Sunshine and Shadow. Pieced quilt, circa 1875.
From Author's collection.

ODD FELLOWS PATCH

TALL PINE TREE

KING DAVID'S CROWN

Odd Fellows Patch. Amish quilt,
circa 1880, based on a five-patch grid.
Author's collection.

Detail of *Odd Fellows Patch.*

CHAPTER VI

Seven-Patch

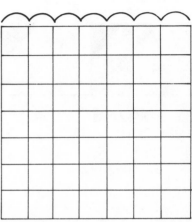

S̲even-patch designs are ones in which the square is divided into a grid of 49 squares or seven equal divisions across the block. This is not a large category and is very similar to the five-patch. The easiest way to draft a 49 square grid is to use the method described in Chapter III. Once the grid has been made most seven-patch patterns can be drafted by connecting the grid lines as can be seen in the designs below.

PRICKLY PEAR

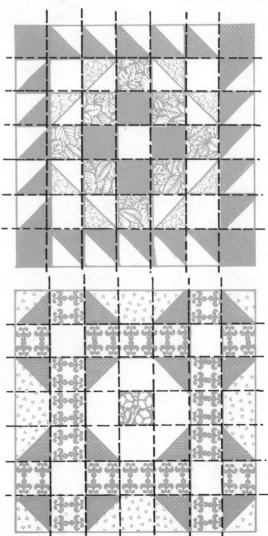

GREEK CROSS

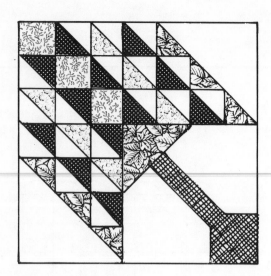

TREE OF PARADISE

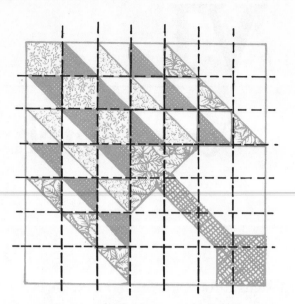

Many seven-patch designs resemble five-patch ones because they consist of a center square and "bars" going to the edge of the block. However, the center divisions are only one-seventh of the width of the square. Instead of the remaining divisions being divided into four squares as in the five-patch, they are divided into nine squares and are treated as a nine-patch. These designs can be drafted either by cutting out individual squares and folding them further, or by simply ruling across the lines of the 49 square grid.

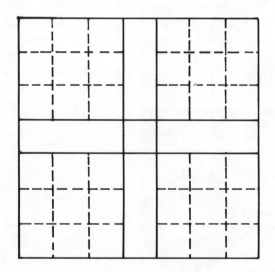

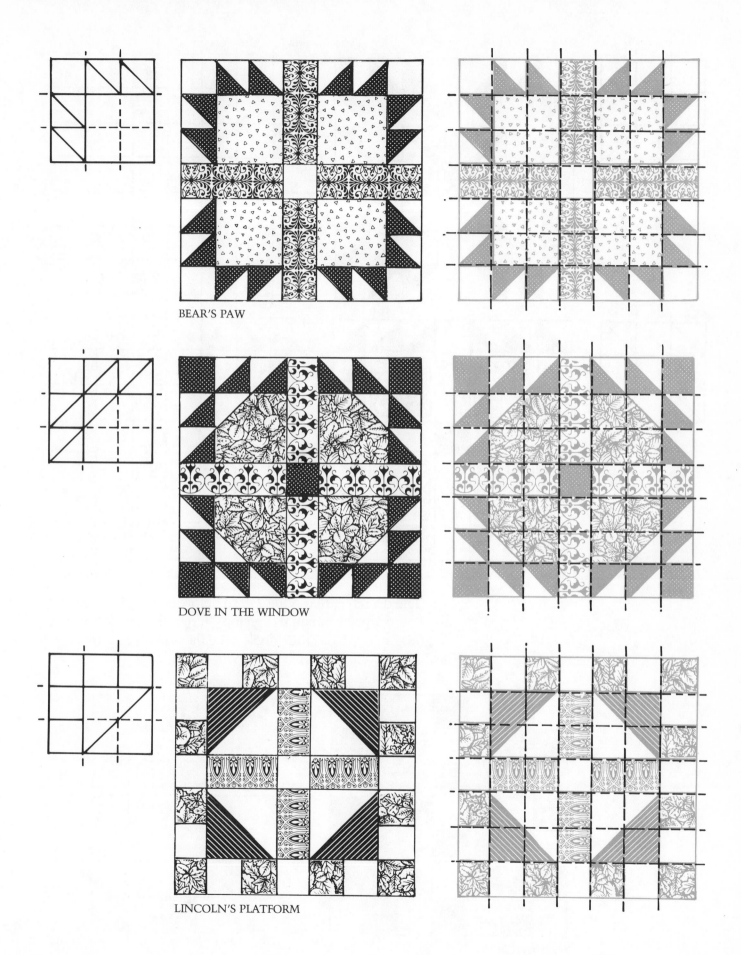

BEAR'S PAW

DOVE IN THE WINDOW

LINCOLN'S PLATFORM

77

PEONY

HEN AND CHICKENS

The design called *Nine-Patch* below is not a nine-patch at all. There are seven equal divisions across the block not three. A grid imposed on the block reveals how the pattern was drafted and shows that it is a seven-patch.

NINE-PATCH

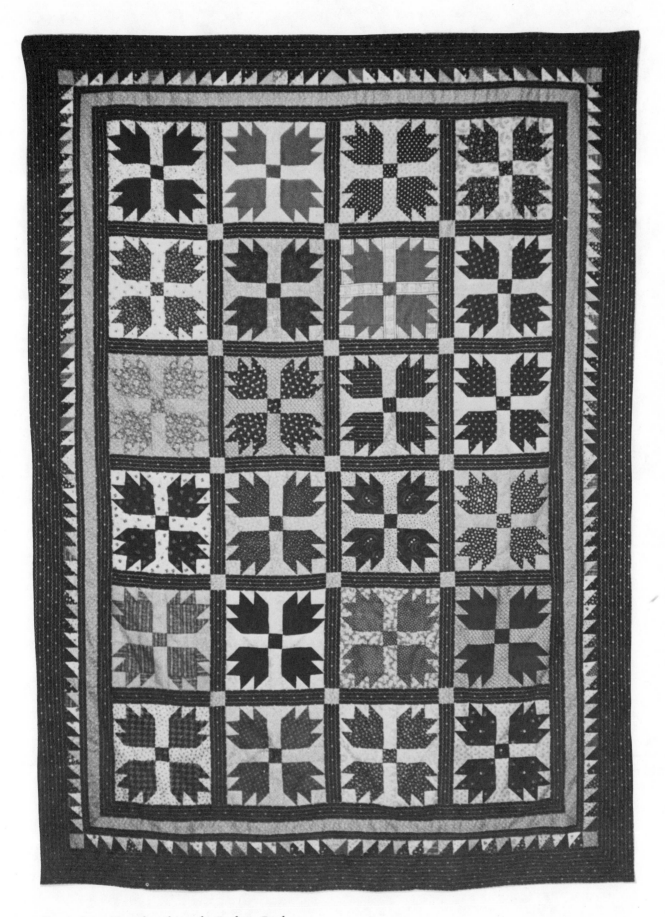

Bear's Paw. Pieced quilt top by Barbara Bockman.

Peony. Pieced and appliqued. Detail of quilt, circa 1840, from the collection of Mary Ann Shindle. The points of the star are made from diamonds taken from the basic eight-pointed star.

Photograph by Steve Thompson.

CHAPTER VII

Eight-Pointed Star

When we hear the term "eight-pointed star," we immediately think of the very basic star. But that is only the beginning of numerous patterns which fit into this category. Once you are able to recognize which patterns fall into the eight-pointed star classification, and to master the techniques of folding and drafting, many design and pattern motifs will emerge which you may never have dreamed you could draft.

The preceding chapters have dealt with dividing a block into equal *squares* and using the grid as a basis for drafting the patterns. If diagonal lines were needed they were made by folding or by drawing across the corners of the individual units. Patterns based on the eight-pointed star are different. They must be drafted by making equal divisions *radiating from the center* of the block instead of using a square grid. These designs are particularly difficult to draft on graph paper because their elements do not fit into one of the basic grids.

When a pattern has three uneven divisions across the top, there is a strong possibility that it is based on the eight-pointed star design. The design falls into the eight-pointed star category when the middle division is equal to the diagonal division across the corner.

Before drafting the actual star, it is better to draft some of of the easier patterns in this category so you can get an idea of the reasoning behind the methods for making this design. There are four different ways to draft an eight-pointed star discussed in this chapter. They are all based on finding the points where the tips of the diamonds touch the edges of the square (points C).

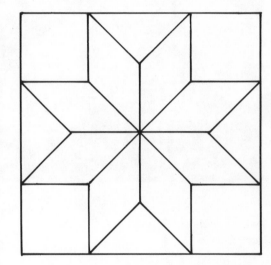

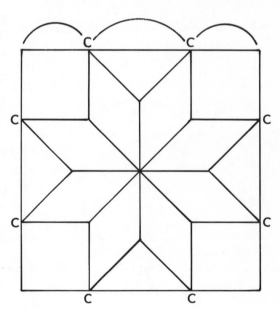

Kaleidoscope. Detail of the color reproduction

Kaleidoscope

The best pattern to start with is the kaleidoscope. This pattern is in the eight-pointed star category because the distance across the center (A) is equal to the distance across the diagonal corner (B). The first question is: "How many pattern pieces are needed?" There are only two: A small corner triangle (#1) and a larger triangle (#2), eight of which form the octagon in the center. The next question is: "How is the square divided?" First take a square piece of paper and try on your own to fold the pattern. As this book has pointed out before, if you work through the pattern yourself, you will remember how it is done much more readily. Gradually you will train your mind to see new and different ways of dividing squares. You will also feel more comfortable about trying to design your own patterns.

If you have not figured out how to fold the paper for the kaleidoscope, look at how it is divided. Most people see eight equal divisions of the square and fold the paper like this:

(Always note where the center of the square is when folding the paper. Be sure the center of your paper is always in the same position as on the diagram. The black dot indicates the center.)

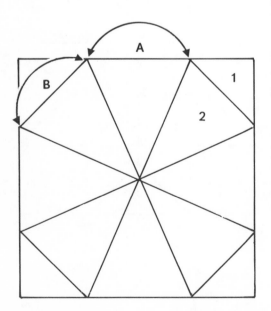

82

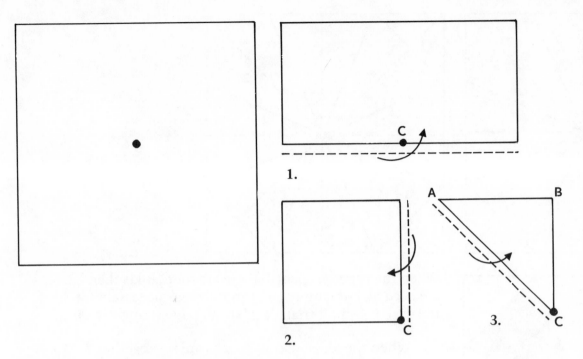

1.

2.

3.

However, when the paper is opened the folds are not going in the right direction.

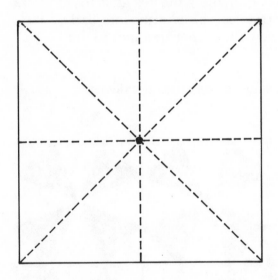

In order to draw the design the paper should be folded to look like this:

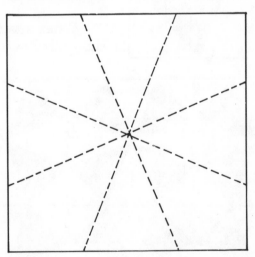

If your paper looked like the first diagram, you did not go far enough with the folds. After folding as in step #3, one more fold needs to be made. Fold edge BC over to meet edge AC. This divides the block into sixteenths.

Finally fold the little flap at the top down along line BD. This will produce the corner triangle.

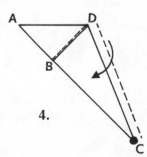

4.

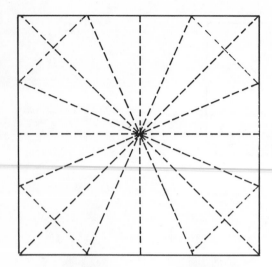

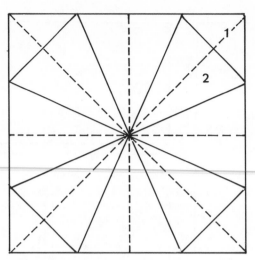

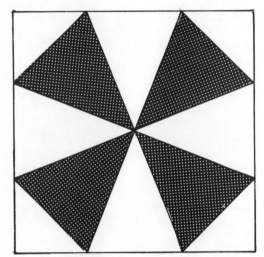

When the paper is opened, there are more folds than are needed, but simply color in the areas necessary for the design—small triangle (#1) and large triangle (#2).

When the kaleidoscope blocks are set together with no setting strips or alternating blocks, some very interesting things happen to the design depending on how the block is colored. One way of making the design is to piece together the large triangles, alternating four darks with four lights, and to sew the corner triangles to the darks.

When several blocks are set together the design shown below emerges.

If it were pieced together in the exactly opposite way with the corner triangles sewn to the lights, the design would look like the one shown below.

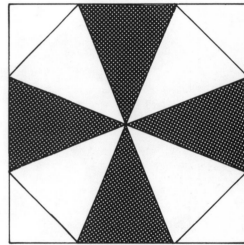

If the blocks were pieced so that each had four darks and four lights, *but* half the blocks had the corner triangles sewn to the darks and the other half to the lights, and then the blocks were alternated in the setting, a totally different design would be made that would look like this:

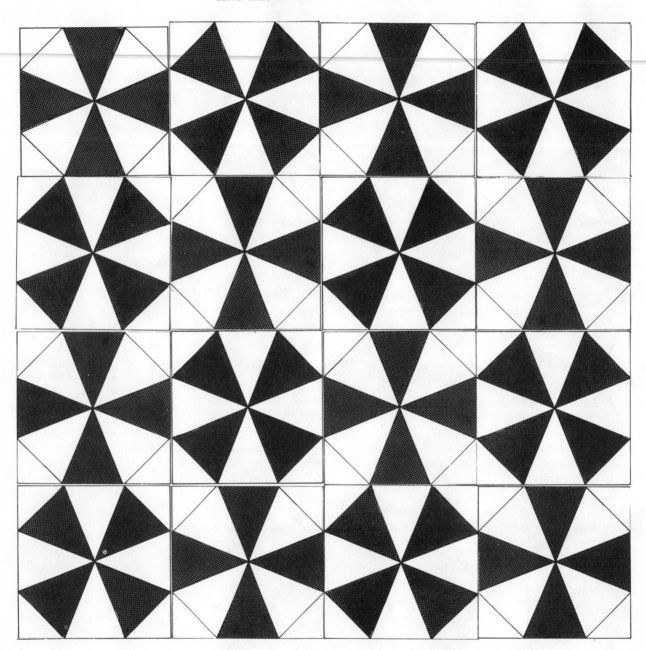

Kaleidoscope Variations

Once the kaleidoscope pattern has been folded, it can then be changed slightly to make numerous other designs based essentially on the same folding procedure, but going a few steps farther.

Variation I Melon Patch

Melon Patch is the same pattern as kaleidoscope. The only difference is that the center octagon is not broken up into triangles, but is cut as one large piece. The design is made so that every other block is the exact opposite in coloring of the block next to it. As an isolated block this pattern is not very exciting, but when nine or more units are put together an interesting optical effect is achieved.

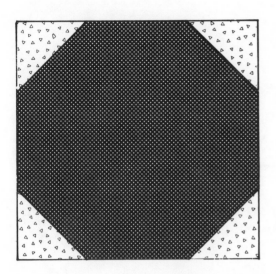
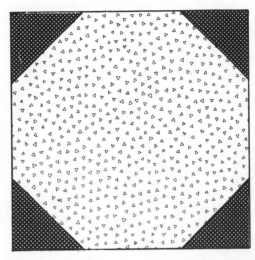

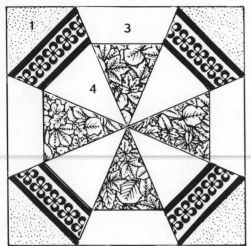

VARIATION II

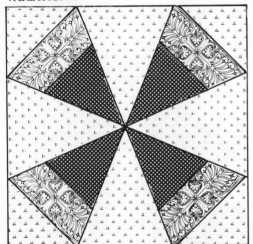

VARIATION III

VARIATION IV SPIDERWEB

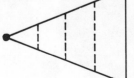

Variation II

Three pattern pieces are needed for this design: Corner triangle #1, triangle #4 and piece #3. The triangle piece #1 is the same corner triangle that was produced by the original folding of the kaleidoscope. For pieces #4 and #3, cut out one large triangle section #2 from the original kaleidoscope and fold it in thirds. In order for the folds to be even, first fold it in half lengthwise, open it out again and use the crease line as a guide when folding the thirds.

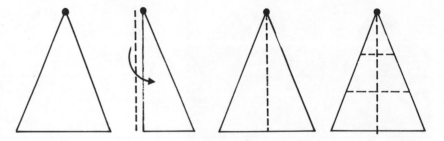

Make template #4 from the top two thirds of the triangle, and template #3 from the bottom third.

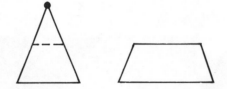

If the kaleidoscope were to be used as a single block for such things as a pillow, apron or wall hanging, this variation would make a much more interesting design than the regular kaleidoscope would if it were used as an individual unit.

Variation III

For this variation simply use four solid triangles of the basic kaleidoscope and four pieced triangles from Variation II.

Variation IV Spiderweb

To make *Spiderweb*, take the basic triangle and fold it into fourths. Make four of the triangles one way, alternating lights and darks, and the other four the opposite. Then, alternate the triangles when you piece the block together. If you want a different effect, make all triangles the same.

Pineapple. Pieced quilt top, circa 1900.
From the collection of Dick and Ellen Swanson.
Photograph by Steve Thompson.

Grandmother's Flower Garden. Pieced quilt of Indian cottons. By Author.
Photograph by Steve Thompson.

SPIDERWEB

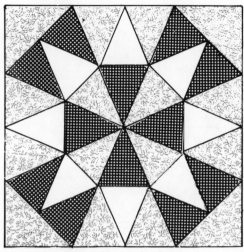

VARIATION V EVENING STAR

Variation V Evening Star

By now it should be apparent that this pattern is based on the kaleidoscope—although it is also an eight-pointed star. The diamonds of the star fit within the triangles of the kaleidoscope. Two pattern pieces are needed: The corner triangle (the same one used in all the kaleidoscope patterns) and a small triangle. To get the small triangle, again start with the large triangle from the basic kaleidoscope.

1. Fold it in half down the middle and open it up again. This fold line serves as a guide to help you fold the rest of the pattern evenly.

2. Fold point C up to point A.

3. Next, crease along lines CB and CD.

4. Open the paper and draw along the fold lines to get the design. One of the smaller triangles will be the second pattern piece needed for *Evening Star*.

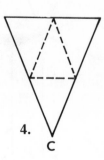

Eight-Pointed Star Method I

A basic eight-pointed star pattern (shown on page 90) can be drafted this way. However, the method I use most is discussed later.

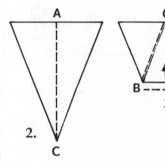

Three pattern pieces are needed for the star: A small triangle #1 (do you recognize that it is the same size and shape as the corner triangle in the kaleidoscope?), a diamond #2 and a square #3. Now look at the *Evening Star* pattern. The triangle in the corner is the same triangle needed for the eight-pointed star. To make the square, (#3), fold a piece of paper. Place the long edge of the triangle along the fold and draw around it. Cut

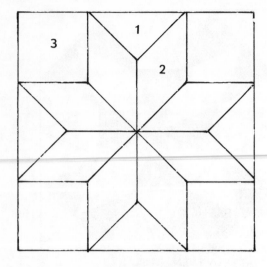

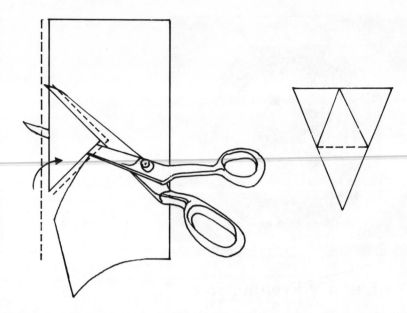

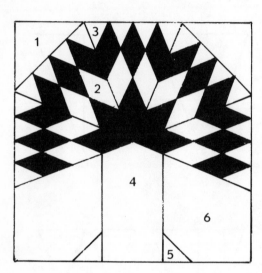

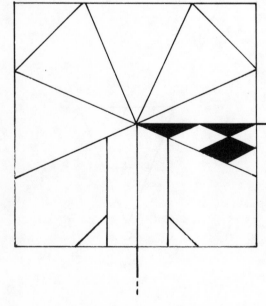

this out, unfold it and you will have the square. Or make the square from the triangle using a triangle ruler as explained in Chapter I. Finally, for piece #2, the diamond, follow the same steps that were used in folding the large triangle to make the small triangle for the *Evening Star*. When the paper is opened, the diamond can be made by drawing along the appropriate lines.

Variation VI Forbidden Fruit Tree

Many of the "tree" patterns are based on the kaleidoscope. *Forbidden Fruit Tree* is no exception. A close look will show that the top portion of the "tree" is composed of five large triangles of the kaleidoscope. Each of those triangles is broken down into small diamonds. Six pattern pieces are needed: Corner triangle #1, small diamond #2, small half diamond #3, large trunk piece #4, small triangle #5 at the base of the trunk, and the pattern piece at either side of the trunk #6. (When cutting the fabric, this piece should be reversed.)

To draft the design, first fold the paper into the basic kaleidoscope. This will produce pattern piece #1 (the same corner triangle in all the kaleidoscope patterns). To make the pieces for the trunk, look at the bottom right quarter of the block and see how that is divided:

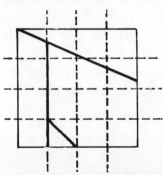

A careful look will show that the quarter section is again divided into fourths which form a 16 square grid, and the side of the tree trunk runs along the first vertical quarter line. The small triangle that forms the base of the tree is the diagonal half of one of the squares of the grid.

1. Cut out one quarter section from the kaleidoscope.

2. Fold it in half lengthwise and then in half again.

3. Open it up and fold it in half and then into quarters in the other direction. (You have taken one quarter section of the folded kaleidoscope and imposed a 16 square grid on it.)

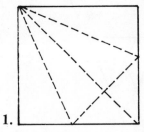

1.

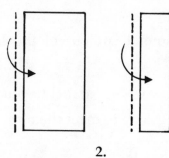

2.

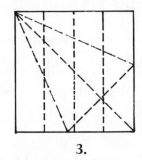

3.

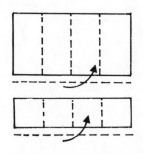

4. Open the paper and rule along fold line AB to get the bottom edge of the tree (This fold is from the original kaleidoscope folding.)

5. Next rule along CD to get the side of the trunk.

6. Finally, rule along EF to get the triangle that forms the base of the trunk.

7. To get the entire trunk pattern, cut out the half trunk section and place it on a folded piece of paper. Draw around it and cut it out. When it is opened you will have the entire trunk shape.

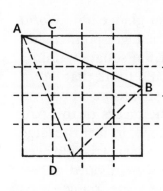

4.

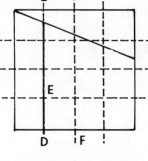

5.

6.

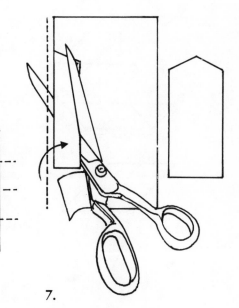

7.

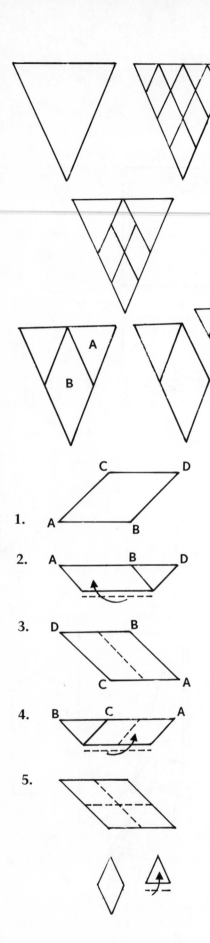

The small diamond #2 and the half diamond #3 are not difficult to make. Cut out one of the large triangle sections of the original kaleidoscope. Look at one individual triangle section of the tree to see how it is divided. A close look will show a larger diamond that has four smaller diamonds within it. Make the larger diamond by following the same steps as for the *Evening Star*, page 89, steps 1-5. Once you have the large diamond, there are two methods to use to further divide it into the small diamond.

Method one is to cut out one small triangle, section A, and fold it in the same method that was used to fold the large triangle to get the large diamond. This will produce the small diamond pattern #2 and half diamond #3.

Method two uses the large diamond cut out of the large triangle:

1. Hold it on the table with two sides parallel to you.

2. Now fold the bottom line AB up to meet the top line CD.

3. Open it up and turn it so the other two sides are parallel to you.

4. Now fold line CA up to meet line DB.

5. Open the paper and you will see that the large diamond is divided into four smaller diamonds. One small diamond is piece #2. For piece #3 simply fold that diamond in half.

Variation VII and VIII
World without End and Blazing Star

It is almost impossible to see at first glance how *World without End* and *Blazing Star* fit into the eight-pointed star category. After reading the definition of the square within a square given in the chapter on it, one would think that *World without End* would fall into that classification. However, there is a direct relationship between the pieces of this particular design and those of the kaleidoscope. In fact the large triangle in *World without End* is the same basic triangle used in the kaleidoscope. If the center square were divided in half diagonally, one quarter of it would be the same triangle used for the corners of the kaleidoscope design.

1. Draft a kaleidoscope. Cut it into quarters.

2. Turn each piece around and put them back together with the corners toward the center.

You will have made *World without End.*

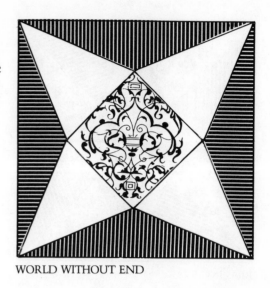

WORLD WITHOUT END

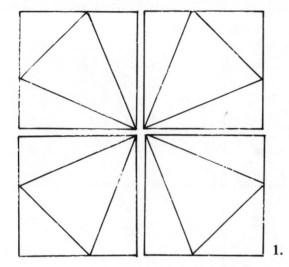

1.

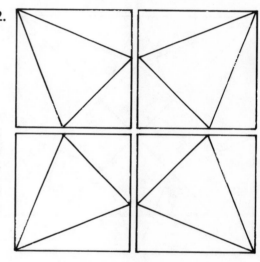

2.

To draft the whole design on paper without having to cut out the pieces, fold the paper exactly as for the kaleidoscope (page 82), *but* after step 3, instead of folding from the center point (line BC over to line AC) as in the kaleidoscope, go to the opposite corner and fold line AB over to line AC. (Note where the center point is.)

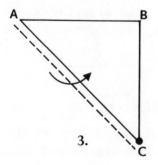

3.

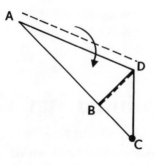

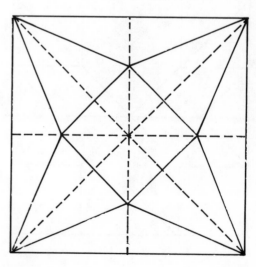

Fold the flap back along BD, and open the paper. Rule along the appropriate lines to get the design.

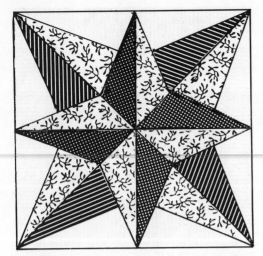

BLAZING STAR

Blazing Star is almost identical. Follow the same procedure as that for making *World without End,* but go a few steps further.

Find the points where the diagonal fold lines from corner to corner of the block touch the edges of the inner square (points A). Next mark the outer edge of the square where it is divided in half (points B). Connect points AB with straight lines as in the diagram to get the other points of the star.

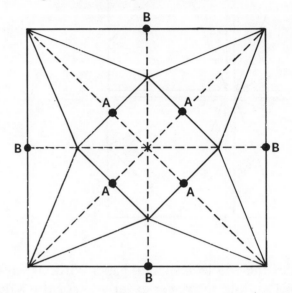

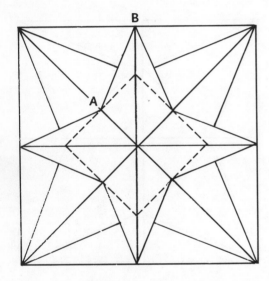

Now that the various kaleidoscope designs have been studied, it may be easier to follow the second method for making the eight-pointed star pattern. I prefer this method over the first because no pieces need to be cut out to get the design and other eight-pointed star variations are easier to obtain from this folding method.

Eight-Pointed Star Method II

Look at the star to see how it is divided. It is easy to see the basic divisions—diagonal from corner to corner and four squares. To get those divisions:

1. Fold the paper in half.

2. Fold it into quarters.

3. Then fold it diagonally.

   Open the paper.

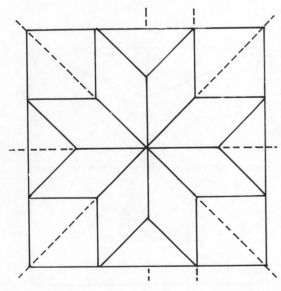

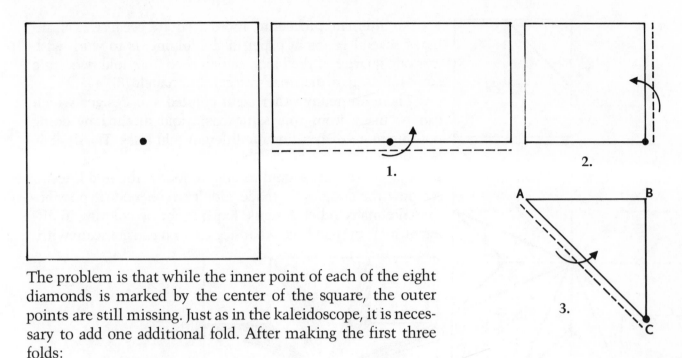

1.

2.

3.

The problem is that while the inner point of each of the eight diamonds is marked by the center of the square, the outer points are still missing. Just as in the kaleidoscope, it is necessary to add one additional fold. After making the first three folds:

4. Fold line BC over to meet line AC.

5. Open up the last fold. The point where the fold line line meets the edge of the paper (D) is the upper tip of the diamond.

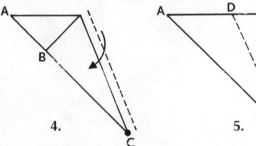

4.

5.

To complete the diamond:

6. Fold center point C up to point D.

7. Now crease along lines DE and DF. Open the paper and there is the star.

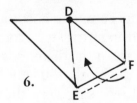

6.

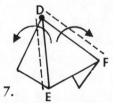

7.

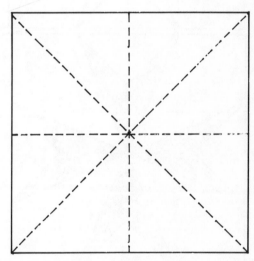

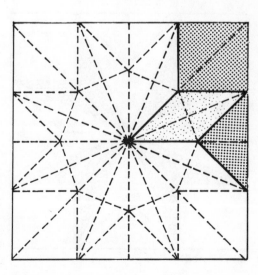

There are more folds than are needed. Simply draw around the large diamonds to get the basic eight-pointed star. You will have all the pattern pieces needed—a large diamond, a triangle and a square.

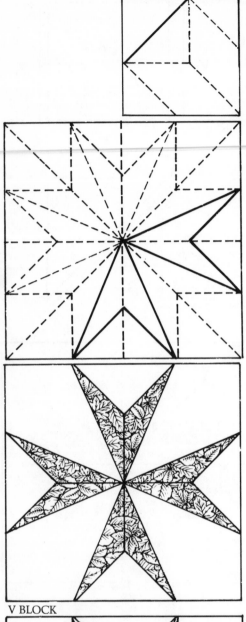

An alternate procedure, more accurate because it eliminates several layers of paper in the folding, is to work with just one quarter of the block and proceed from fold two. Rule across the square diagonally to get the triangle (8).

There are many other eight-pointed star designs which can be made from this same basic fold method by doing nothing more than ruling on different fold lines. The designs below are some examples. By looking at the fold diagram for the star above, you should be able to follow the fold lines to see how the designs are made. Don't stop here. It is possible to make many other designs. Experiment by coloring in different fold lines and see what designs you can come up with.

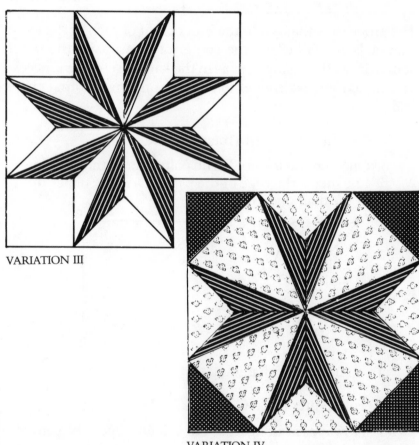

VARIATION III

VARIATION IV

V BLOCK

SILVER AND GOLD

I find that many of my students complain about a lack of accuracy when folding for the eight-pointed star—sometimes the corners are not absolutely square or the diamonds are not even. By folding only a quarter of the block, thus eliminating several thicknesses of paper, and by using very thin paper, I feel that this method can be quite accurate. However, there are two other ways to draft the star: Either use partial folds and a ruler or make *no* folds, but use a compass and a ruler. These methods are very accurate and are not difficult.

Eight-Pointed Star Method III

If you look closely at the eight-pointed star, you will see that if straight lines were drawn connecting the outer tips of the diamonds—skipping two diamonds each time—the sides of the diamonds would be formed. Therefore all that is needed is to find the outer tips of the star. To do that:

1. Fold the paper into sixteenths as for the beginning of the kaleidoscope or as for either of the eight-pointed star fold methods, steps 1-4. When the paper is opened you will see this:

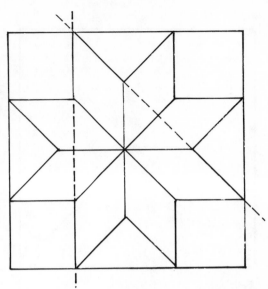

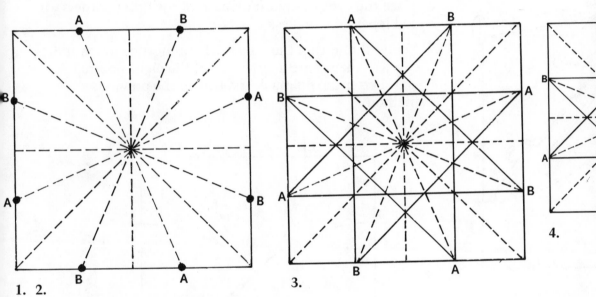

1. 2.

3.

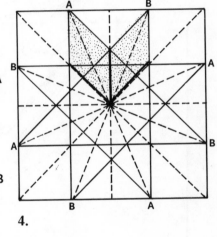

4.

2. Now, working clockwise from the upper left edge, mark the folds that represent the tips of the diamond with letters AB—one A and one B along each edge as in the diagram.

3. Next draw straight lines connecting the AB points. Do not connect an A with an A or a B with a B—only draw lines from an A to a B.

4. Rule along the original fold lines to complete the centers of the diamonds.

There are several other designs which you can make by coloring in different portions of the folded and ruled lines used in this method.

One such design is *St. Louis Block*.

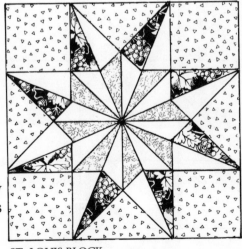

ST. LOUIS BLOCK

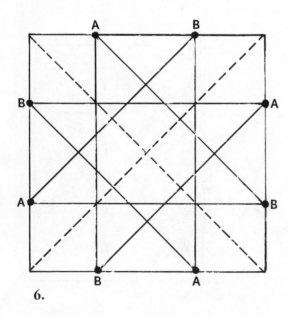

1.

2. 3.

6.

Eight-Pointed Star Method IV

If you still feel that the initial folding into sixteenths is not accurate enough, the star can be drafted without folds by using a compass and a ruler.

1. Find the center point of the square. This can be done by drawing lines diagonally from corner to corner.

2. Next take a compass, place the point on one corner, and open it out until the pencil reaches the center of the paper.

3. Draw an arc with the compass that cuts through two sides of the square. Draw lightly so that the pencil only marks the edge of the paper.

4. Place the compass point on each of the other corners and repeat the process.

5. You will find that the points where the arcs touch the edges of the square are the tips of the eight-pointed star. Letter the points A and B as in the previous method.

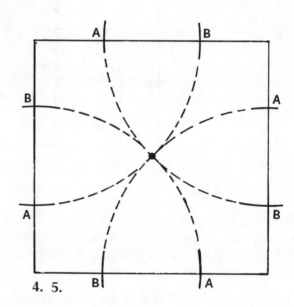

4. 5.

6. Form the star by following steps two and three of Method I.

98

7. To finish the diamond, draw straight lines dividing the block into a four-patch. There are already diagonal lines from corner to corner. These lines will form the rest of the diamond.

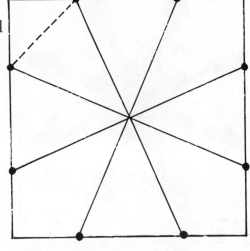

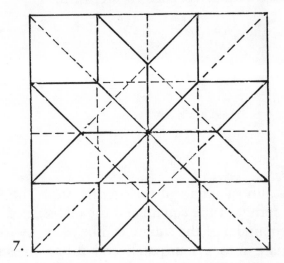

7.

The kaleidoscope can be drafted in the same way. Once all the points have been marked around the edge of the block, draw lines from one point to the point diagonally across from it on the opposite edge of the paper. Connect the dots across the corner to get the corner triangle.

Many times the eight-pointed star is seen "turned" with one of the points straight up. *Evening Star* (page 89) is one version of this, as well as the design at the right.

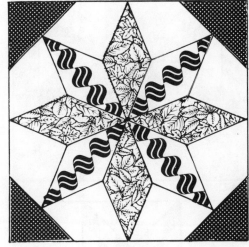

Methods III and IV can be used to draft this star as well. The A and B points must again be marked, but this time the letters are shifted so that points A are on the quarter fold lines and points B on the diagonal fold lines where they intersect the corner triangles. The A and B points are connected as in the other methods.

There are many quilt patterns based on the eight-pointed star which require going on beyond the basic drafting methods. For some of the designs, a diamond of the star must be cut out and then folded further.

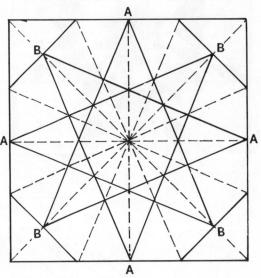

VIRGINIA STAR

Virginia Star

In the *Virginia Star* each diamond is divided into four smaller diamonds. Divide the diamond by the same method as was used for *Forbidden Fruit Tree*, page 90, steps 1-5.

Blazing Star

Blazing Star is almost identical to *Virginia Star*. The small triangle in the corner of the square and the odd-shaped piece which is the remainder of the square can be made by folding the corner square into a four-patch and ruling diagonally across one of the small squares. Rule diagonally across the corner square to get the other edge piece needed for the design.

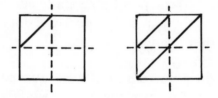

BLAZING STAR

Harvest Sun

The *Harvest Sun* is the same basic eight-pointed star. This time, however, the larger diamond is divided into nine smaller diamonds. The same procedure can be followed as for the *Virginia Star*, but the diamond must be folded into thirds each direction instead of halves.

Follow the same procedure for making even larger starburst patterns such as the *Lone Star*. Start out with a bigger piece of paper (if you can't find paper big enough you can work from one quarter of the design as explained previously) and keep folding the diamond as many times as you wish.

The next group of eight-pointed star patterns are ones in which the points of the star do not touch the edge of the block. These have a smaller eight-pointed star drafted in an inner square. These are not as complicated as one might think and close study of some of them should give you the knowledge of how to deal with any you may encounter.

HARVEST SUN

Harvest Sun. Quilt made by Elizabeth Williams, 1833.
From the collection of Dick and Ellen Swanson.

ROLLING STAR

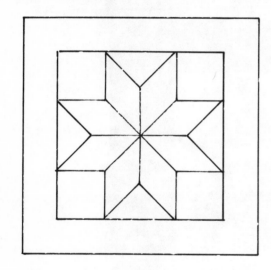

Rolling Star

Three pattern pieces are needed for *Rolling Star:* A triangle #1, a square #2 and a diamond #3. An eight-pointed star can readily be seen in the center of the block. That star fits into an inner square. But the question is: How do you find that inner square? First look at the overall block. You can see that points A and B are the tips of an imaginary eight-pointed star covering the whole square. The corner triangles are the same corner triangles that are formed when the kaleidoscope is drafted. Therefore:

1. Fold the paper into a kaleidoscope. This will produce the corner triangle (#1) for the first pattern piece. Mark the point where the diagonal fold line touches the corner triangle with "C."

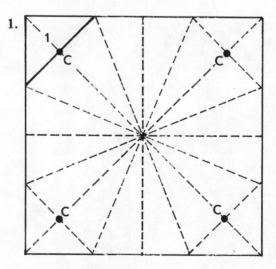

2. Connect points C with straight lines to get the inner square.

3. Connect points D (quarter fold lines) with straight lines. (All you are doing here is making a square within a square as was done in the four-patch chapter.)

This will produce the diamond piece #2 needed for the pattern. This outer diamond is the same size piece as the inner diamond, so there is no need to draft further. If you are skeptical, draft an eight-pointed star in the inner square and compare the size of the outer to the inner diamond. They will be the same.

The last piece needed is a small square for #3. A close look at the inner square will show a small kaleidoscope with corner triangles. One of those smaller triangles is *half* the square which is needed. The square can be completed by either 1) completing it with a draftsman's triangle, or 2) connecting directly opposite points "E" with straight lines (4).

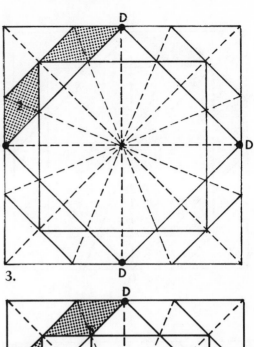

3.

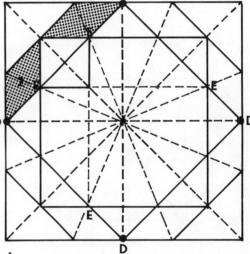

4.

Star and Chains

This variation is identical to *Rolling Star* except for one more row of patterns around it. The method for getting the pattern is almost identical. Five pattern pieces are needed: Large corner triangle #1, large diamond #2, smaller triangle #3, square #4 and small diamond #5. There are two ways to draft this pattern.

Method I

To get the pattern using Method I it is necessary to find two inner squares.

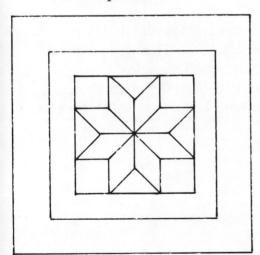

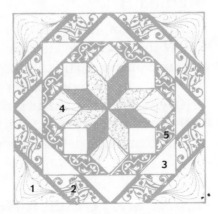

STAR AND CHAINS

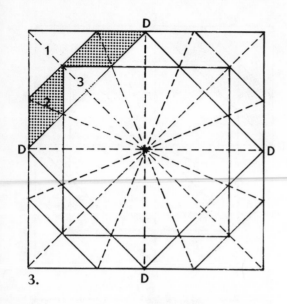

3.

1. and 2. Same as steps one and two in *Rolling Star*.

3. Connect points D. This will produce larger outer diamond #2, and the small triangle #3. The corner triangle is already there from the basic folding.

4. Next find point E where the diagonal fold lines cross the center of triangle #3. Connect points E. This will produce the smaller inner square.

5. Finally, make a "square within a square" in the larger inner square by connecting points "F." This will produce the smaller diamond #5. This is the same diamond as the one in the center eight-pointed star, so there is no need to draft further.

6. To get the square piece #4, follow the same procedure as for *Rolling Star*, page 102, method 1 or 2.

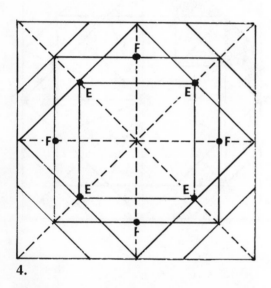

4.

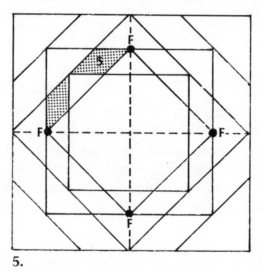

5.

Method II

Perhaps a simpler method of drafting *Star and Chains* is to follow the first three steps for *Rolling Star*. This will produce the large diamond and the large and small triangles.

Next cut out one quarter section from the original piece of paper. (The inner square is the same size as a quarter section of the total block.) Draft an eight-pointed star in this square to get the remaining pattern pieces.

Double Star, Dutch Rose or Broken Star

The pattern for this design can be made in two ways.

DOUBLE STAR, DUTCH ROSE, BROKEN STAR

Suzi's Box. Pieced quilt of Indian cottons by Author. The design is based
on a hexagon and was adapted from a mosaic box owned by Suzi Golan.

Photograph by Steve Thompson.

Inner City. Quilt top based on hexagon. By Author.
Photograph by Steve Thompson.

Method I

Look at the eight-pointed star in the center of the block. It is the same size as the eight-pointed star in the center of *Star and Chains*. Only three pattern pieces are needed: A square #1, a diamond #2 and a triangle #3. As was done with *Star and Chains* the block can be divided into fourths and an eight-pointed star can be drafted in one quarter section. This will produce all the pattern pieces needed—a diamond, a square and a triangle.

Method II

If imaginary lines are drawn forming the large diamond of an original eight-pointed star, you can see that diamonds A and B are part of a larger diamond that is the same as the diamonds in *Virginia Star*. (Diagram 1.)

    Therefore the first step is to draft an eight-pointed star, cut out one large diamond section and fold it to get four smaller diamonds as was done for *Virginia Star* on page 100. One of the smaller diamonds will be the pattern piece needed for #2. Next take the corner square of the large eight-pointed star and fold it into a four-patch. One of the four small squares will be pattern piece #1. To get the triangle for piece #3, fold the small square in half diagonally. (Diagram 2.)

Lemoyne Star

The *Lemoyne Star* is another pattern where a center square is needed for the eight-pointed star. It is the same inner square which was needed for *Rolling Star*. By following the first three steps for *Rolling Star*, you can get the diamond of the inner star as well as the larger triangle. Or, if you prefer, draft the inner square in the same way as for *Rolling Star* and then draft a star within the square.

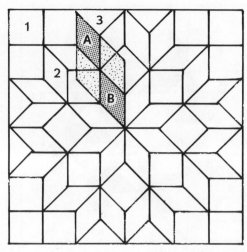

1.

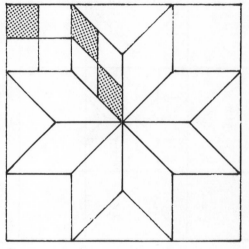

2.

LEMOYNE STAR

FLYING SWALLOWS

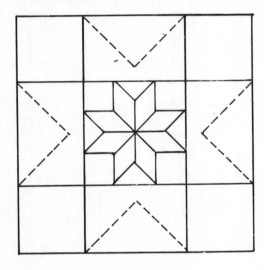

CASTLE WALL

The diamonds in the corners are actually part of a small eight-pointed star. A close look will show that if the star were complete it would cover one fourth of the paper. So, to get the pattern pieces fold the original block into a four-patch, cut out one quarter section and draft an eight-pointed star in it. This will produce the small diamond, square and triangle for the small eight-pointed star.

The only other piece needed is the rectangle. If the square from the small eight-pointed star is doubled by putting two of them side by side, it will form the correct shape and size piece needed for the rectangle.

Flying Swallows

One can readily see the large eight-pointed star in *Flying Swallows*, but there are three points of a smaller eight-pointed star within each diamond of the larger star. If the inner corners of the squares of the eight-pointed star are connected, the lines will produce a smaller square in the center of the block.

Close study of the partial small star in the design will show that if it were whole it would fit into that center square. Therefore all that is needed to finish making the pieces of the pattern is to:

1. Draft a large eight-pointed star on a paper of the size needed for the complete design. This will produce the large square and triangle.

2. Form the center square by connecting the inner corners of the squares in the star.

3. Draft an eight-pointed star in the center square. That will produce the small diamond and small triangle which are needed for the remaining templates.

Castle Wall

Castle Wall is a beautiful pattern when pieced, but few people attempt it because they cannot find a pattern and it seems impossible to draft. However, you will find this complicated pattern well worth the concentrated efforts required to understand it and to draft it. Five pattern pieces are needed for the design—corner triangle #1, shape #2, square #3, diamond #4 and inner triangle #5.

To draft the pattern:
1. Take a close look at the design. Points A are the tips of an eight-pointed star, so the basic star must be drafted first.

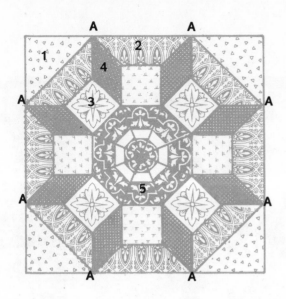

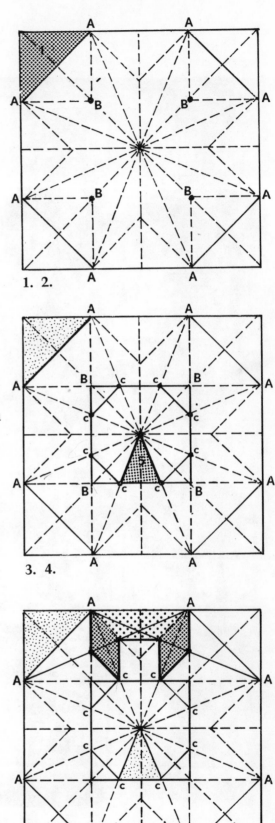

2. Draw diagonal lines connecting points A across the corners of the block. This forms the same corner triangle as in the kaleidoscope and is piece #1.

3. Now study the diagram of *Castle Wall.* You will see that the triangles in the center form an octagon which is part of a smaller kaleidoscope. The center square must first be found in order to get the octagon. This can be done by connecting the inner corners (B) of the corner squares of the eight-pointed star. (This is the same square which was needed for *Flying Swallows.)*

4. Now, connect points C with straight lines diagonally across the corner of the inner square to get the inner octagon as well as the remaining triangle pieces #5.

5. The next step is to find the diamond. The outer tips of the diamonds are at points A and the inner tips are at points C. The top angles of the diamonds are formed by the angle of the large diamonds of the original star. But in order to complete the small diamond, it is necessary to find the halfway mark between the two tips A and C. That mark can be found by connecting every other point A as in the diagram. You will find that the line cuts directly through the middle of the small diamond. Rule from point C up to where the line you just drew between points A intersects the original diamond and the smaller diamond will be formed. Once two of the small diamonds are formed, three sides of a square will be apparent. Close off the square—piece #3—by drawing a line across the top. This will also produce the last piece needed, shape #2.

Log Cabin, Courthouse Steps. Pieced quilt top, circa 1920. From the collection of Dick and Ellen Swanson.

Photograph by Steve Thompson.

CHAPTER VIII

Patterns with an Isolated Center Square

There are many designs with a square in the center that has no relation to the rest of the block. That square can either be "square-set" or "diagonal-set." Sometimes the squares are extended to the edge of the block in either diagonal bars going to the corners or in vertical or horizontal bars going to the sides. The square in these designs does not need to be a specific size—if it were, the design would most likely fall into one of the other categories.

Most nine-patch designs have a square in the center, but that square is one-third of the total block, as in *Ohio Star*.

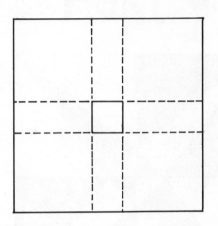

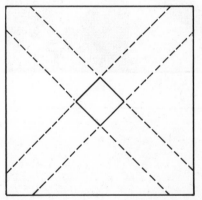

OHIO STAR

In four-patch designs, the relationship of the center square to the rest of the block is easily seen and may be described by a fraction such as one-fourth or one-eighth, as in *Rising Star*.

RISING STAR AND SQUARE

109

GOOSE TRACKS

LOG CABIN

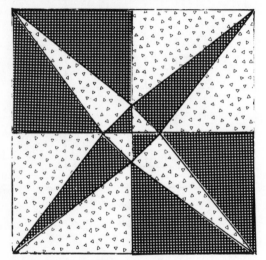

CROSSED CANOES

With five-patch designs, the center square is always one-fifth of the width of the total block, as *Goose Tracks*.

But what about the *Log Cabin?* It has a square in the center that is not always related to the logs going out from it.

Crossed Canoes is another pattern which has an isolated square in the center—although this time it is a diagonal square.

"Square-Set" Squares

Any time a design is encountered that has an isolated "square-set" square in the center, the square can be obtained by following these procedures:

1. Take a piece of paper that is the size of the square you want and fold it diagonally.

2. Next fold side AD down to meet side CB.

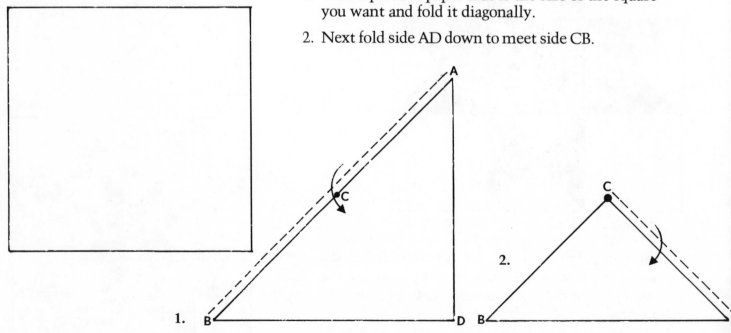

3. To get a square in the center of the block, all that is needed is to fold the center point "C" down. *However*, in order to insure that the fold for the square will be straight, first crease the triangle in half lengthwise, by bringing line CB over to meet CD. Open the paper.

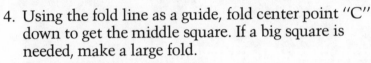

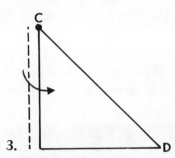

4. Using the fold line as a guide, fold center point "C" down to get the middle square. If a big square is needed, make a large fold.

   If a small square is needed fold a small portion of the corner down.

5. Open the paper to see the square.

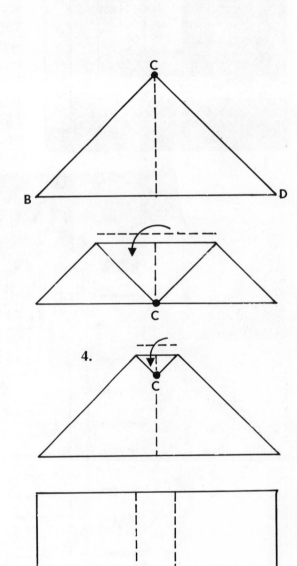

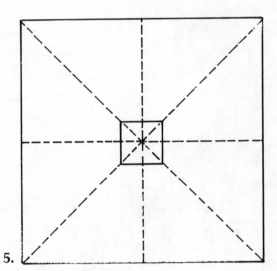

6. If the pattern needs bars going from the square to the edge of the paper, place the ruler along the sides of the inner square and extend the sides to the edge of the block.

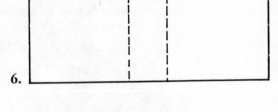

Log Cabin

The *Log Cabin* is, perhaps, one of the most popular of all quilt patterns. The design is built around a "square-set" square in the center of a block. One way of piecing the *Log Cabin* is to use no pattern, but to build strips around the square, cutting them off as they reach the edge of the center unit. The block grows until the number of units to be added have been sewn on. However, this method is not exact and it will be difficult for you to predict the finished size of the block. What if a certain size is needed to fit a quilt or other project? It is necessary to know how to draft the pattern. It is

Log Cabin, Courthouse Steps. Detail. *Photograph by Steve Thompson.*

112

also important to cut individual templates. If strips are sewn on and then cut off when they reach the edge of the center unit, the block is apt to get wavy around the edges and not to lay flat.

Careful study of different log cabin patterns shows that there is always a square in the middle which appears to be totally isolated from the rest of the block. The square may be large or small. It does not have to be the same size as the "logs," or twice the width of the "logs." In addition to the middle square, there are almost always four logs. Each log is parallel to one side of the square.

This pattern cannot be divided into a four-patch or nine-patch, and does not seem to fit into any other category. However, now that you know how to get a square in the middle of a piece of paper, you should also be able to figure out how to get the logs. Take a square of paper and try it.

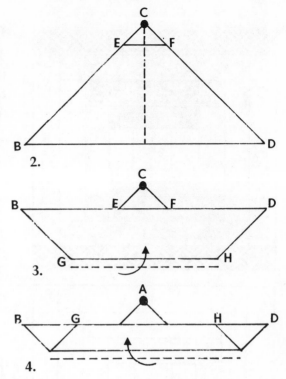

1. Follow the first four steps for getting a "square-set" square in the middle of the paper.

2. Lift up the "flap", C, of the center square.

3. Fold edge BD up to meet line EF.

4. Next, fold the section in half again by bringing line GH up to meet line EF. The top triangle (the center square) has been ignored, and the remaining portion has been folded into fourths.

5. Open the paper to see the guidelines for drawing the pattern.

Extend the vertical sides of the center square to the first fold to make the first pattern piece. Then extend the horizontal sides of the rectangle formed by the center square and the first pattern piece to make the second pattern piece. Working clockwise, keep extending the sides of the center (the center grows as you continue) out to the next fold until the edge of the block is reached.

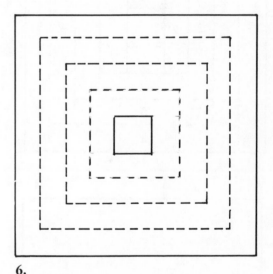

When piecing this design, pattern pieces one and two will be of the same "light" fabric, pieces three and four of the same dark fabric and so on. Even though there are sixteen "logs," sixteen templates are not needed. Careful study will show that number one is the only piece of its size. However, pieces two and three are the same size, as are each two pieces after them up to numbers fourteen and fifteen, although each pair is progressively larger. The very last piece, number 16, is the only one of its size.

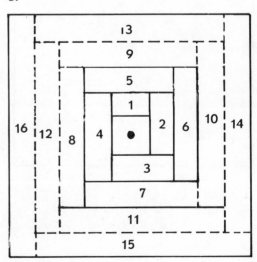

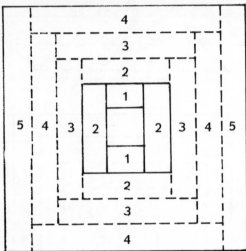

Courthouse Steps

The *Courthouse Steps* variation of the *Log Cabin* is made a little differently. Instead of being built up clockwise around the center square, the block is made by adding logs to the opposite sides of the center.

1. Extend the vertical edges of the center square out on *both sides* to the next fold. That will produce the first pattern piece.

2. Draw the square formed by the first fold lines and you will have the second pattern piece.

3. Continue building logs opposite each other on all sides until the paper has been filled.
   Once again, templates for each log are not needed. The templates for logs #1 and #5 are used twice; each of the other templates are used to make four logs.

Diagonal-Set Squares

Some patterns have a "diagonal-set" center square instead of a "square-set" one. These squares, too, often have "bars" that extend to the edge of the block, except, unlike the bars of the "square-set" ones, the bars of these run diagonally. To draft a "diagonal-set" square:

1. Fold the paper into a square.

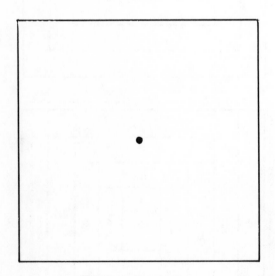

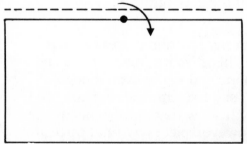

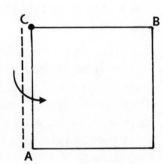

2. Make a diagonal crease to use as a guide so that you will be able to fold the center square evenly. (Fold side CA over to meet side CB.)

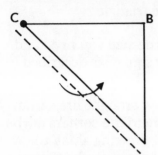 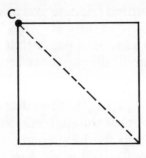

3. To form the center square, fold center point "C" over to meet the crease line. Once again, if a large square is needed, make a large fold. If a small square is needed, make a small fold.

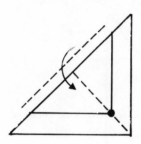 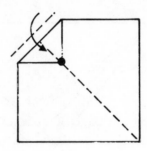

Open the paper.

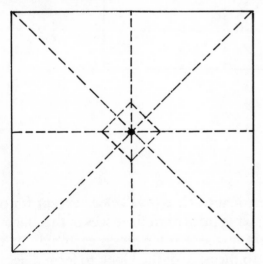

4. If diagonal bars are needed, place a ruler along the side of the square and extend the lines out to the edge of the paper.

A rule to remember is: If a "square-set" square is needed, fold the paper diagonally. If a "diagonal-set" square is needed, fold the paper into a square.

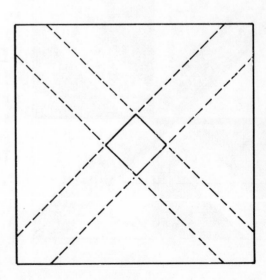

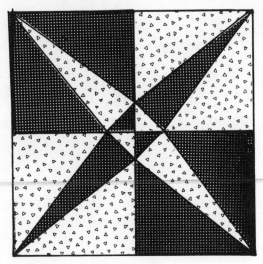

CROSSED CANOES

Crossed Canoes

Crossed Canoes is a design with a diagonal-set square in the center which has no relation to the size of the block. It can be large or small. Three pattern pieces are needed—a center triangle, a long pointed triangle and a wide triangle.

1. Cut out a piece of paper that is the size you need and draft a small diagonal-set center square as described above.

2. Open the paper. With a ruler draw straight lines from the corners of the diagonal square to the corners of the block to get the long triangle. By drawing along the fold lines in the square you will have all the pattern pieces needed for the design.

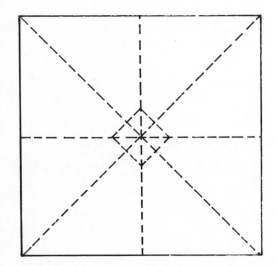

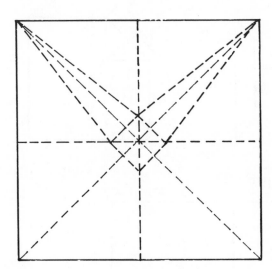

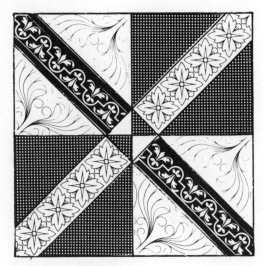

DEVIL'S PUZZLE

Devil's Puzzle

Devil's Puzzle is identical to *Crossed Canoes* except for one change. Instead of drawing lines from the edges of the diagonal square to the *corners*, place a ruler along each side of the square and extend it to the edge of the block to form diagonal bars.

116

Center Square Designs Combined with Another Category

There are some patterns which are a combination of the "Square in the Center" category and another category. For example, *King David's Crown* looks like a combination of a "square-set square" with bars going to the edge and a "diagonal-set square" that is similar in design to *Crossed Canoes*, page 110.

However, a closer look will show that the square in the center is one seventh the width of the design so that it is first necessary to draft a 49 square grid as for the seven-patch designs. Once you have the grid, fold the paper again to make a diagonal-set square, then draw lines from the edges of the square to the corners of the block to get a design similar to *Crossed Canoes*.

With these grids of two categories imposed on each other, it is then possible to color in the appropriate lines for the design.

Mexican Rose

Mexican Rose is another design which is made from a combination of two categories: It is drafted by using the grids for the eight-pointed star and a diagonal-set square. Six pattern pieces are needed for the design. To draft the pattern:

1. Take a piece of paper that is the size you want the finished block to be and draft an eight-pointed star on it.

2. Next connect the inner points of the triangle in the star (points A) with straight lines to get a large diagonal-set square.

KING DAVID'S CROWN

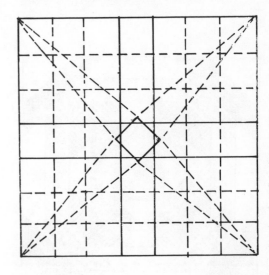

MEXICAN ROSE   MEXICAN CROSS

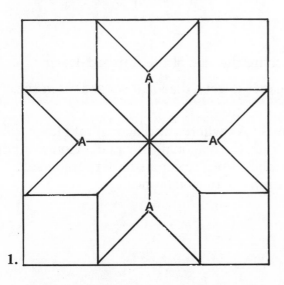

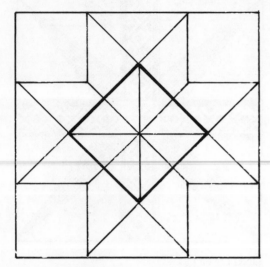

2.

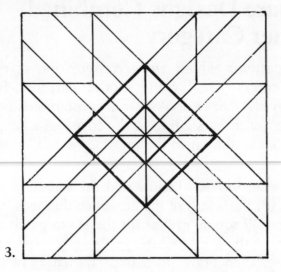

3.

4.

PINEAPPLE

3. Fold the paper to get a small diagonal-set square in the center and extend the edges of this square to the edges of the block to make diagonal bars across the block.

4. By drawing along the appropriate lines, you can get all the pattern pieces needed for the design.

Pineapple

The *Pineapple* is a complicated pattern which is related to the *Log Cabin*. Both a square-set square and a diagonal-set square can be seen in the center of the design. A study of different pictures of the *Pineapple* will show that the squares in the center can be large or small. The strips surrounding the squares can be various in number. The method for drafting a pattern that has four strips is described below, but the pattern can be altered to use however many strips you like.

Method I

1. Make a square the size of the finished design.

2. Fold the paper to get a diagonal-set square in the center.

3. Mark points "A" where the diagonal fold lines intersect with the diagonal-set square. Connect points A with straight lines to get a smaller square-set square within the diagonal one.

118

Pineapple. Pieced quilt top in wools and silks, made by Vera Bycraft, circa 1875. Ypsilanti, Michigan. From the collection of Dick and Ellen Swanson.

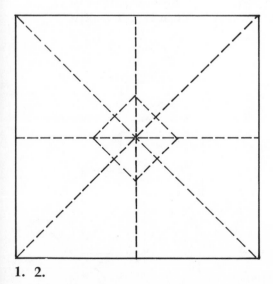
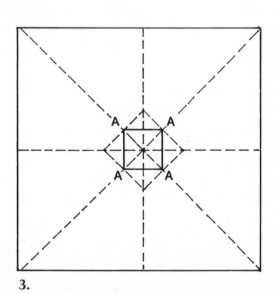

1. 2.

3.

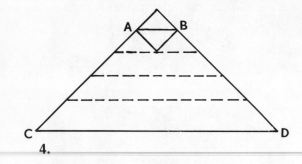

4.

4. Follow the directions on p. 113, and fold the paper into a *Log Cabin*, using the square-set square as the center. (The distance between line AB and line CD will be folded into fourths.)

5. Open the paper. Mark the fold lines lightly with a pencil.

6. Using a compass, measure the length of the quarter fold from the edge of the square-set square to the edge of the paper.

7. Move the compass and mark off the same distance from the corner of the square-set square along one of the diagonal fold lines (point C).

8. Fold the paper into a four-patch.

9. Fold the diagonal-set center square forward along line AB, which is the side of the diagonal square, and, using the diagonal fold line as a guide, fold the opposite corner forward along point C.

10. Ignoring the two "flaps" which have just been folded in, fold the rest of the paper (the length of the arrow) into fourths.

11. Open the paper and mark the folds lightly with a pencil.

12. Now you have the guidelines for the *Pineapple*. Starting with the diagonal-set square and working diagonally toward the corners of the paper, mark the lines as in the diagram.

Once all the corners are marked, it is easy to see and to mark the rest of the design.

Note: Folding paper as many times as this method requires may cause some loss of accuracy in the grid unless the paper is extremely thin. A more accurate method is discussed below.

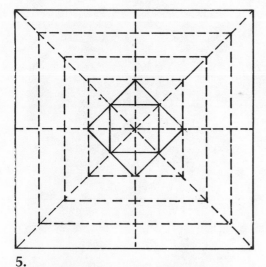

5.

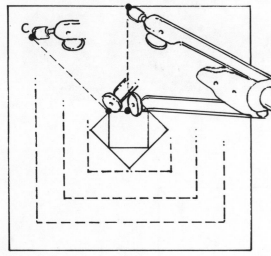

6. 7.

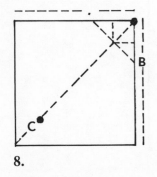

8.

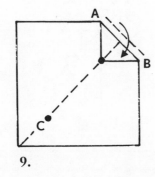

9.

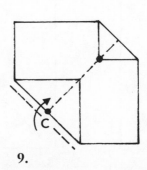

9.

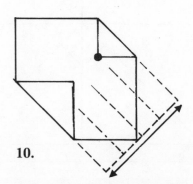

10.

120

Hexagon wall hanging. By Author.
Photograph by Timothy Janaitis.

Bicentennial. "Sampler" pieced quilt. The central motif is based on a
five-pointed star. By Author.

Photograph by Steve Thompson.

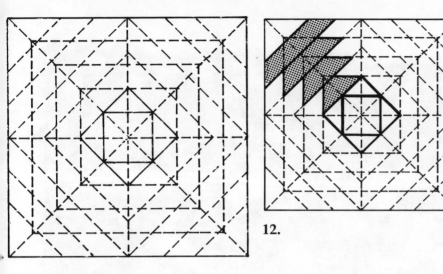

12.

Method II

A reliable way to draft this pattern exactly is to use the method described in Chapter III to divide an area into equal units.

1-3. Follow the same first three steps as the above method to get the squares in the middle of the paper.

4. Using the method described in Chapter III, divide the distance between the edge of the inner square-set square and the edge of the paper into fourths. Do this on all four sides.

5. Using a triangle for accuracy, lightly draw in the divisions to form boxes around the center square.

6. Follow steps 6 and 7 in method I, but mark the distance on all four diagonal fold lines.

7. Again, using a ruler and the method described in Chapter III, divide into fourths the distance just marked along all the diagonal fold lines.

8. Using a triangle, draw in the divisions forming boxes around the diagonal-set squares.

9. Finish the design as in step 11 of the previous method.

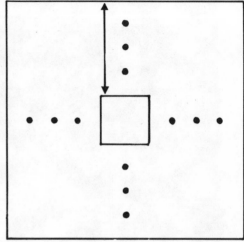

4.

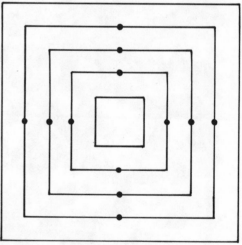

5.

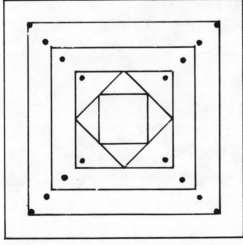

6. 7.

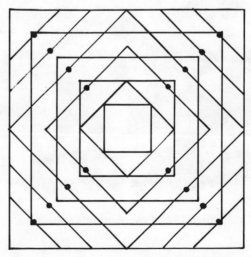

8.

121

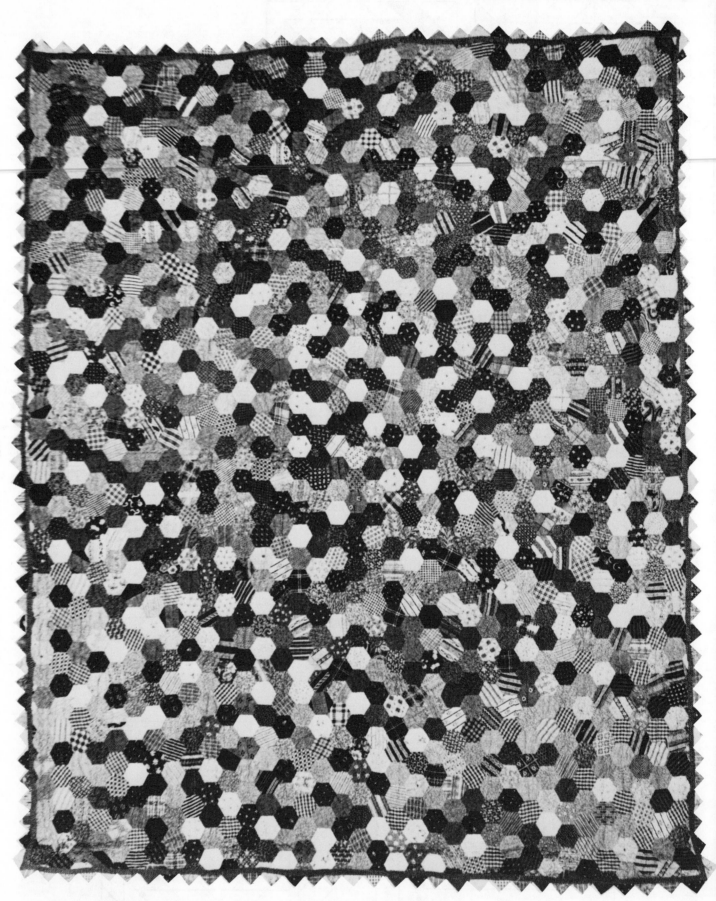

Honeycomb. Quilt, circa 1870, from Author's collection.

CHAPTER IX

Hexagon

The hexagon is one of the oldest forms of geometric patchwork. Patterns using the hexagon and its variations have always been extremely popular in England. Elaborate hexagonal configurations of diamonds and triangles have been used for centuries in Islamic Art, and hundreds of mosaic designs based on the hexagon can be found in buildings and mosques throughout the Middle East. I find it one of the most exciting and versatile shapes to work with.

The basic hexagon was, perhaps, first put together in random fashion. This version was called *Honeycomb* (see photo opposite). As quiltmakers grew more imaginative, they began to design secondary patterns and the most popular of all hexagon variations emerged in the *Grandmother's Flower Garden*. This pattern is one in which the hexagons form rosettes: Usually, the center is one color, a circle of six hexagons around it is a second color and a third circle of 12 hexagons is made of yet another fabric. Individual "flowers" are made until there are enough for the quilt. Then they are arranged and sewn together with either another row of hexagons or a row of diamonds as the "setting" pieces.

Another version of the flower garden is that where, instead of rosettes, diamonds are made as in the diagram below.

GRANDMOTHER'S FLOWER GARDEN

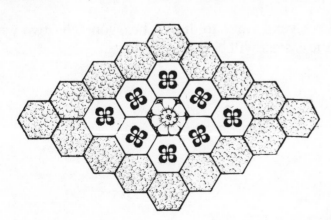

The diamonds can then either be put together in rows or in the form of large stars throughout the quilt.

There are several ways to draft a hexagon. The two which I feel are the easiest will be discussed here.

Hexagon Method I

1. Decide how big you want the hexagon to be and draw a circle that size. Fold the circle in half.

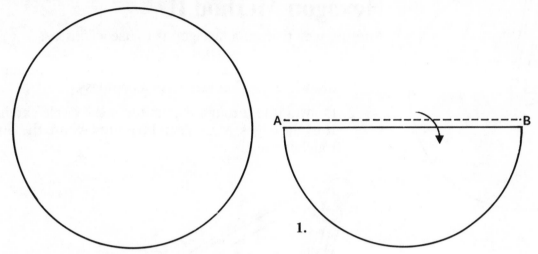

2. Find the center of the circle (the center of line AB) by folding A over to B and pinching the center point C. *Do not crease the entire circle.* Open again to the half circle.

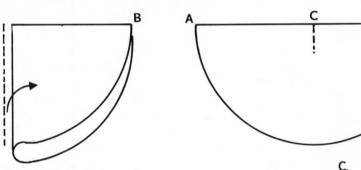

3. Starting at center point "C," fold the half circle into thirds to get wedges shaped like pieces of pie.

4. Rule across points DE and cut along the ruled lines. Open the paper and you will have the hexagon.

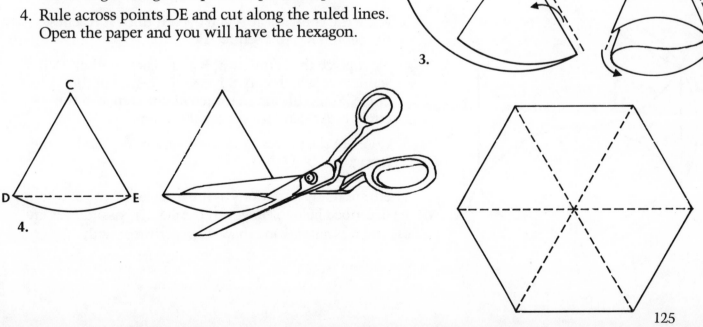

Hexagon Method II

Another way to draft a hexagon is to use a compass.

1. Decide what size you want the hexagon to be and draw a circle that size with a compass.

2. Draw a line through the center of the circle extending it to the edges. Mark A and B points where the line touches the circle.

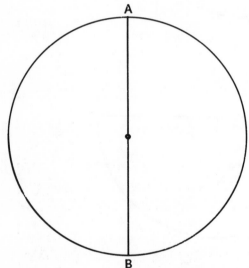

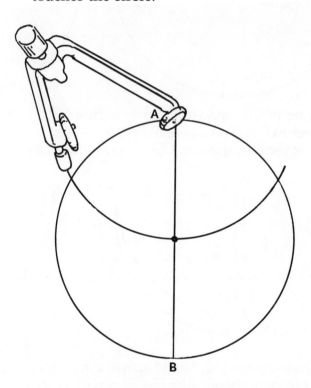

3. Place the compass at A and open it until it reaches the center. Make a semicircle.

4. Next place the compass at B and make another semicircle which cuts through the center of the circle. You will find that the circumference of the circle is divided into six equal sections.

5. Connect the points as in the diagram to complete the hexagon.

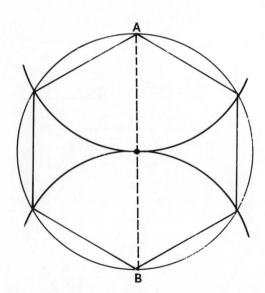

There are many variations of the hexagon, some of which wil be described below. However, the design possibilities are endless and it is an exciting shape to experiment with.

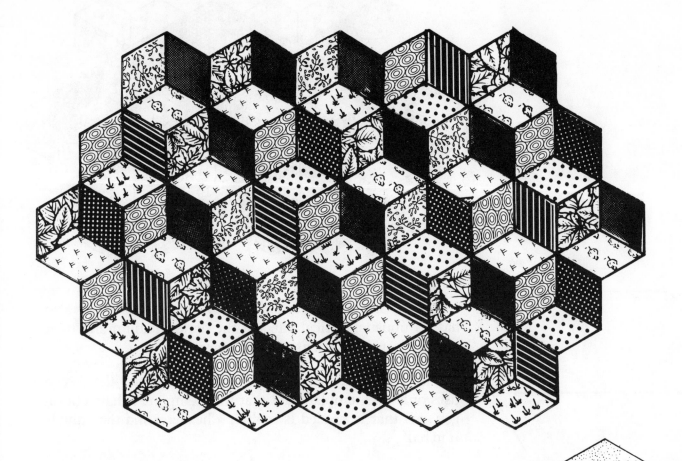

Tumbling Blocks

If you look closely at the *Tumbling Blocks* pattern, you will notice that it is made up of three diamonds which form a hexagon. With consistent use of dark, medium and light fabrics, an optical effect occurs which makes the blocks look as if they were stacked on top of each other.

To achieve this effect, dark fabrics must always be in one position, lights in another and mediums in the third. If you are not careful with the color placement, stars may emerge instead of blocks. A variety of fabrics can be used when piecing this as long as care is taken to sort them into darks, mediums and lights, and they are pieced together according to the rule. To draft this pattern:

1. Draft a hexagon employing either method I or II. If you used method II, connect opposite corners of the hexagon with straight lines. If you used method I, the lines are already on the paper.

2. The hexagon will be divided into six triangles. Two of the triangles form the diamond that is needed for the pattern.

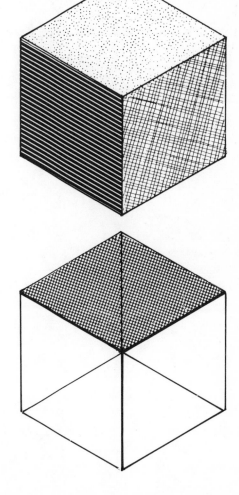

Inner City

Inner City is a design similar to *Tumbling Blocks* which also has an unusual optical effect if the dark, medium and light pieces are used in a consistent manner.

A close look at this pattern will show that the design uses only one template and that that template is half a hexagon. All that is needed is to draft a hexagon and then divide it in half.

The design is pieced in "y-shaped" units keeping the darks on one side, the mediums on another and the lights on the third.

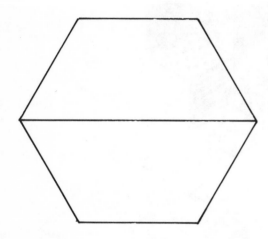

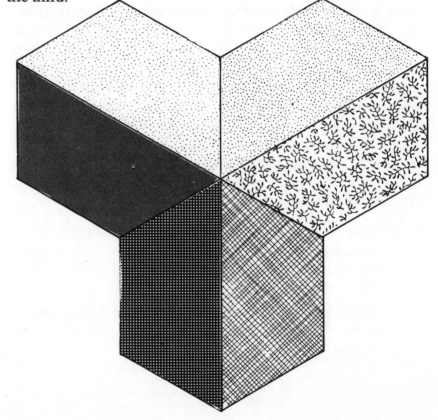

Six-Pointed Star

Six-pointed stars drafted within hexagons make interesting patterns. There are two types of patterns that are composed of six-pointed stars fitted into a hexagon: In one the points of the star touch the *sides* of the hexagon (star #1), and in the other the points of the star touch the *corners* of the hexagon (star #2).

Six-Pointed Star #1

To draft this type of star:

1. Make a circle of the desired size. Using either method I or II draft a hexagon within the circle. If method I were used, you should not unfold the paper; leave it in the triangular shape. If method II were used, you should fold the hexagon into a triangle.

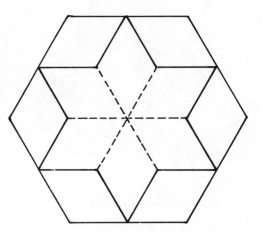

STAR #1

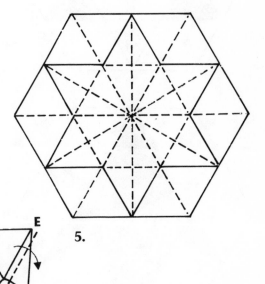

STAR #2

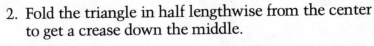

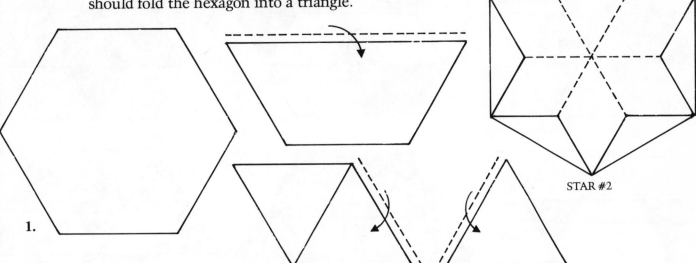

1.

2. Fold the triangle in half lengthwise from the center to get a crease down the middle.

   Open it up.

3. Now fold center point C down to meet crease line B.

4. Next crease along lines DB and EB.

5. Open the paper to see the star.

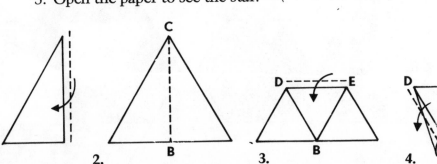

2.   3.   4.   5.

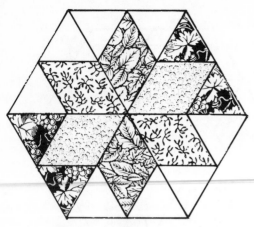

There are many patterns that can be developed from this one simple method of folding. It is merely a matter of looking at the folds and coloring the areas desired to make a particular design. Pictured below are only some of the designs that it is possible to create using the folds of the first six-pointed star.

Star #1 Variations

Six-Pointed Star #2

Two methods will be shown for drafting the second six-pointed star: One requires a ruler and the other requires folding.

Method I

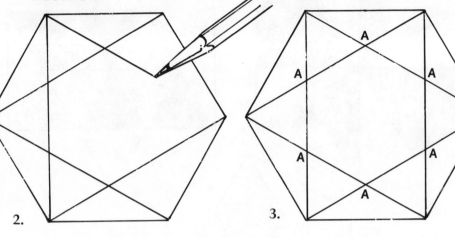

2.   3.

1. Draft a hexagon.

2. Connect the corners of the hexagon with straight lines following the diagram opposite.

3. Connect the "A" points which are opposite each other with straight lines to finish making the diamonds in the star.

Method II

This star can also be made by folding.

1. Draft a hexagon and place it in the same position as in the diagram.

2. Fold point A down to point B.

3. Fold point E down to line BG so that corners D and B match up exactly.

4. Next fold F over to H.

5. Fold center point C down to point B.

6. Crease along lines IB and JB to finish the star. Below are a few of the designs that can be made from the fold lines of this method.

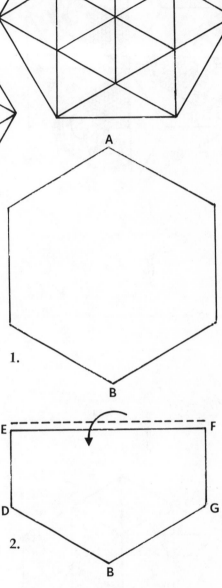

1.

2.

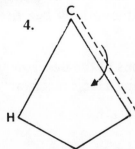

3.

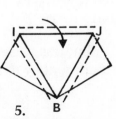

4.

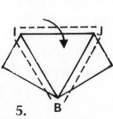

5.

131

Star #2 Variations

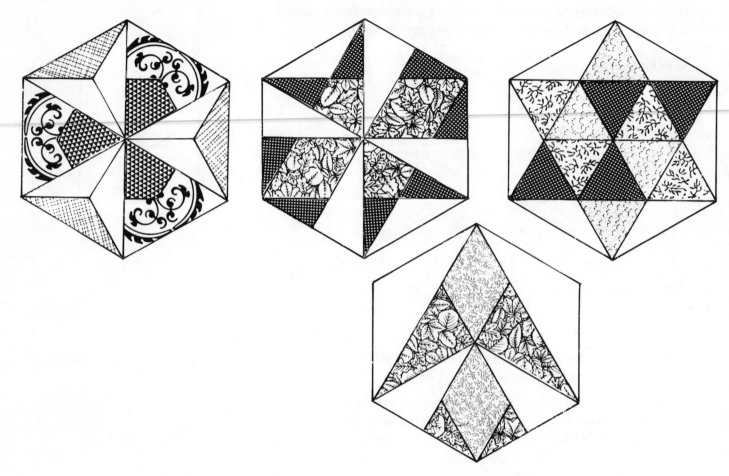

Six-Pointed Star 1 and 2 Combined

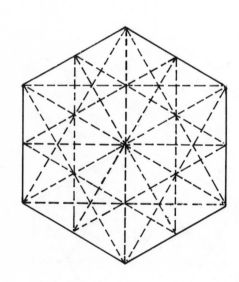

Some very exciting designs can be created by drafting *both* six-pointed stars on the same hexagon. Make a large hexagon and try it. I find it is easier to see new designs when the paper-folding method is used for drafting the stars. Later, when actually making the templates, you may then want to use a ruler and compass for more accuracy. When both stars have been drafted on the same paper, the hexagon will have lines on it as in the diagram below.

Hold the paper at an angle and squint. Depending on the way the light shines on the folds, different designs will appear. Below are a few of the designs that can be obtained from drafting both stars on the same hexagon. It is fun to try to make different configurations because the possibilities are unlimited.

Endless variations of the hexagon are possible. It is fun to experiment by making a large hexagon "grid." Cut a very large

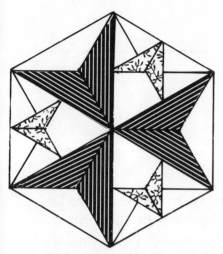
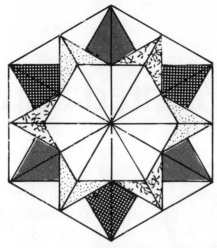
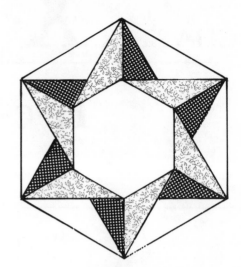

circle from newsprint and fold a hexagon containing a star #1. Once the star has been folded, do not open the paper, but fold the triangle down again as if making another star. When the paper is opened, you will find many triangles on the hexagon. By coloring in different ones, you can make a variety of designs.

The hexagon can be folded down as many times as you like to get even more triangles on the surface. It should be noted that, with so many folds, a template would not be made from those triangles; but for experimentation with design, folding is the quickest way to get a large "grid" on the paper.

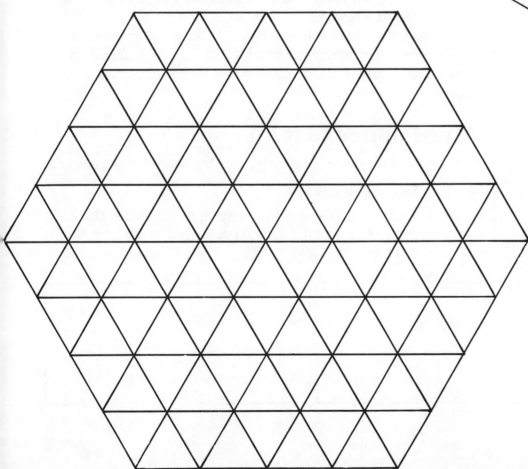

CHAPTER X

Five-Pointed Star

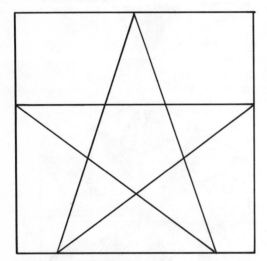

FIVE-POINTED STAR #1

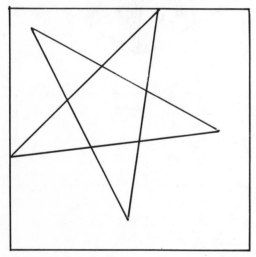

FIVE-POINTED STAR #2

During our nation's Bicentennial, many people made quilts to commemorate the birth of the United States and the five-pointed star became a popular motif. However, since 1976 and before that time, the five-pointed star has largely been put aside as a basis for quilt designs. I feel that the five-pointed star is a form of geometric design which has not been fully explored for patchwork, and that there are some possibilities for "new discoveries" in quilt designs stemming from the lines formed when this star is drafted.

It is possible to draft a five-pointed star by making a circle and marking off every 72 degrees on the circle with a protractor. However, when I am experimenting with new designs, I prefer using the fold methods described below because they are faster to make and there are more lines to use as an aid to discovering new designs.

Two methods of folding the paper for a five-pointed star will be discussed here: One in which the star is centered on a square and another in which the star is set in one corner of the square.

Five-Pointed Star #1

1. Make a square of the size that you need for the design.

2. Fold the square in half.

3. Next divide the left-hand edge into thirds. Do this either by using the method described in Chapter III or by folding (Chapter IV).

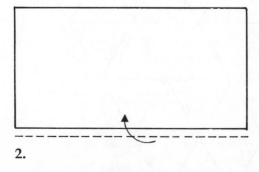

2.

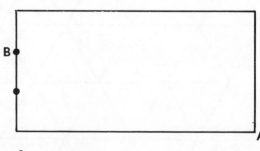

3.

4. Bring the lower right corner (A) up to the top third mark (B) and crease.

5. Fold line CD over to line BD.

6. Fold line ED forward to meet line FD.

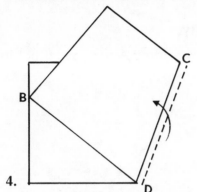

4.

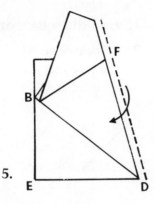

5.

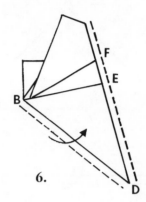

6.

7. One way to make a star now is to put a crease in the paper from point "E" to somewhere along line BD as in the diagram.

When the paper is opened, the star will be there. However, the points are apt to be to fat or too skinny. To get a perfectly symmetrical five-pointed star it is better to follow steps 8, 9 and 10 below.

8. If you want a perfect star, do not follow step 7. Instead, open the paper. You will see that it is divided into 10 sections. Hold it as in the diagram with the line dividing the square in half perpendicular to you and the point where all the divisions meet toward the bottom of the paper.

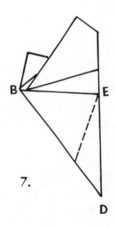

7.

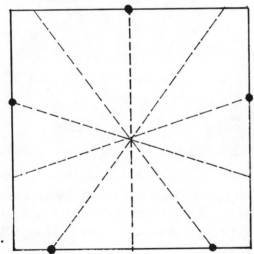

8. 9.

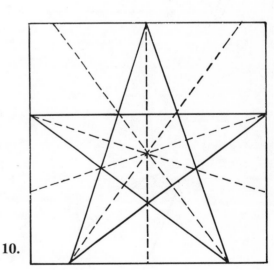

10.

9. Now, starting with the top middle fold and working clockwise, make a dot on every other fold as in the diagram.

10. Draw straight lines connecting every other dot to form the star.

Five-Pointed Star #2

This five-pointed star is not square on the paper, but set in one corner. The method for drafting it is very similar to the previous one.

1. Fold the square diagonally.

2. Divide edge AC in half by folding A to C and pinching the halfway mark (D).

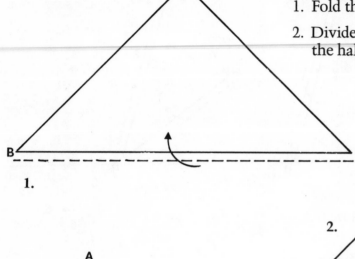

1.

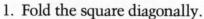

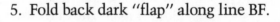

2.

3. Fold B up to D.

4. Next fold line EF over along line BF.

5. Fold back dark "flap" along line BF.

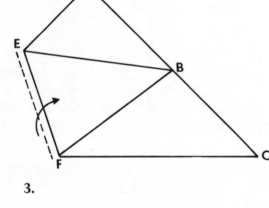

3.

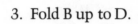

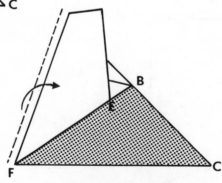

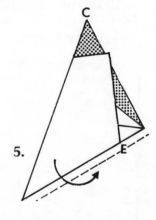

4.

5.

6. Once again you can fold the entire star by making a crease from point "E" to somewhere along line CF. However, to get a perfect star, it is better to continue on to steps 7 and 8.

7. If you have not done step 6, put your thumbnail at point E and make an indentation with your nail.

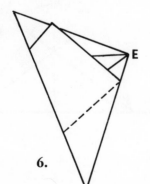

6.

Detail of *Sunflower* quilt.
Photograph by Steve Thompson.

Sunflower. Pieced quilt of Indian cottons by Author.
Photograph by Timothy Janaitis.

Open the paper and hold it on the diagonal so that the line which cuts the block in half diagonally is perpendicular to you. Starting at the top, make a dot on every other mark where your fingernail made an indentation as in the diagram.

8. Connect every other dot as in the diagram below to get the star.

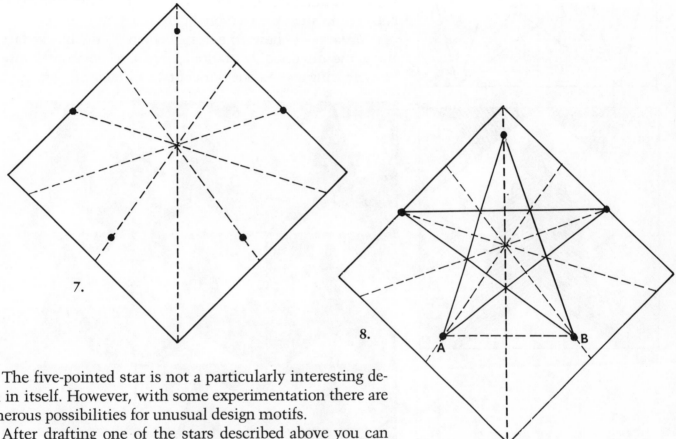

The five-pointed star is not a particularly interesting design in itself. However, with some experimentation there are numerous possibilities for unusual design motifs.

After drafting one of the stars described above you can work with the fold lines on the square. Place a thin piece of paper over the diagram and color in certain folds until you have a motif that you like. One square in itself will not be very interesting, but when you combine four or more blocks, the interaction of the shapes creates an entirely new surface design. Experiment with the placement of the blocks. The five-pointed star pattern does not have a symmetrical repeat of the elements within the block as do most other geometric designs. Therefore, if the star in one block is pointing up and in another is pointing down, there will be a completely different design than if all the blocks were pieced together with the star pointing in the same direction. Below are some designs I have developed from this concept. Read how they have been made and then have fun experimenting with five-pointed star designs on your own.

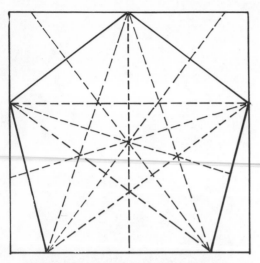

Designs Based on Five-Pointed Star #1

Design 1

After the basic star #1 was drafted, the points of the star were connected with lines that formed a pentagon within the square. A thin piece of paper was then placed over the drawing and certain areas were colored in to make this design.

Variation 1 shows the design when all the blocks face in the same direction. Variation 2 has one horizontal row of blocks facing up and one horizontal row facing down.

VARIATION 1

VARIATION 2

Design 2

This design was made with the same star #1 as was used in design 1. However, different lines of the diagram were colored in to achieve the following effect.

Variation 1 shows the effect created when the blocks are pieced together with one row pointing up and one row pointing down, and variation 2 shows what happens to the design when the same blocks are pieced together with the star pointing alternately up and down.

VARIATION 1

140

VARIATION 2

141

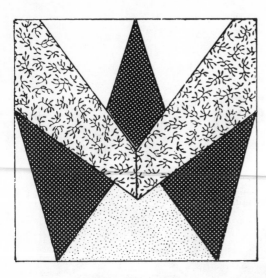

Design 3

Design 3 shows yet a third version of star #1 where the portions have been colored in to achieve the following effect.

Again, totally different surface designs occur when the blocks are placed with one row up and one row down as in variation 1, or when they are placed with one block up and one block down alternately as in variation 2.

VARIATION 1

VARIATION 2

Designs Based On
Five-Pointed Star #2

The next three star designs are based on Star #2 which is set in the corner of the square. The elemental design of this star seems to be expressed best when four blocks are used as a unit. Place the blocks within the unit so that the same corner of each block points toward the center, or so that two blocks point toward the center and two point away from it.

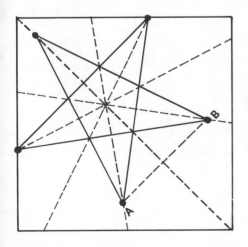

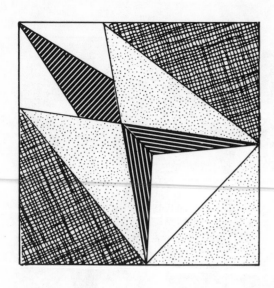

Design 4

This design is made by drafting star #2 and then coloring in areas according to the diagram below. The only additional line comes by connecting two of the fold lines (A and B) with a straight line. The design is then put together in units of four blocks that have the same corner pointing toward the center.

When you put units composed of four of the blocks side by side, an interesting design occurs as seen in variation 1. Variation 2 shows a different design that appears when you place together units of four blocks, two of which have the points facing out and two of which have the points facing in.

VARIATION 1

VARIATION 2

Designs 5 and 6

These are created by coloring in different areas of star #2, as was done to make design 4. Once again these have been put together in units of four with the same corner on each block facing the center of the unit.

It should be noted that different designs may be created by placing the blocks in different arrangements. However, simply changing the coloring of the blocks will also create a totally new effect.

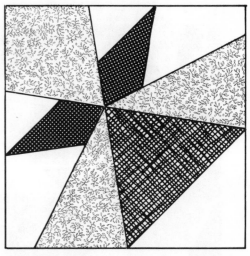

DESIGN 5

DESIGN 6

DESIGN 5

FIVE-POINTED STAR DESIGN 6

CHAPTER XI

Curved Patchwork Patterns

There are many curved seam patchwork designs. I have tried in this chapter to present an overview by dealing with various ones that will prove to be similar to others you may encounter. Once the basis for constructing these patterns is recognized, understanding how to draft and to design others will become readily apparent.

Most designs with curves are actually based on patterns which fall into some of the other categories. You first have to see the underlying "grid" and then place the pattern in the correct category. For instance, the following curved patterns fall into the four-patch category.

ORANGE PEEL

"Four-Patch" Curved Patterns

Orange Peel

To draft *Orange Peel*:

1. First divide a square of paper into the basic four-patch. Mark the point where the fold lines reach the edges of the paper with dots (A).

2. Place the point of the compass on one of the dots and open it out until the pencil hits the center of the paper. Draw a half circle with the compass.

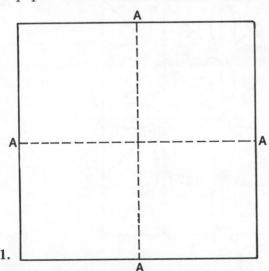

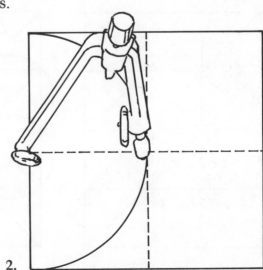

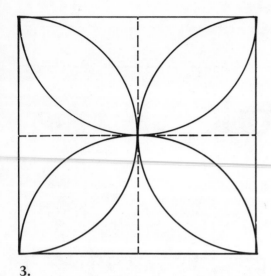

3.

3. To complete the design, place the compass point on each of the other three dots and repeat the process.

Winding Walk

Winding Walk is also a four-patch design. This time, however, a 16 square grid is needed.

1. Ignore the curves on the design, divide the block into 16 equal squares and make the underlying design by ruling diagonally across the appropriate squares.

2. In order to make the proper size circles, it is necessary to find the centers of each of the squares. To do this, divide the squares diagonally from corner to corner.

3. Place the compass point in the center of each of the squares which have been divided diagonally. Open it until the pencil reaches one corner of the small square, and make circles. Color in the portions needed for the design. You will have more circles than you need.

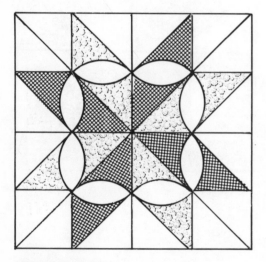

WINDING WALK

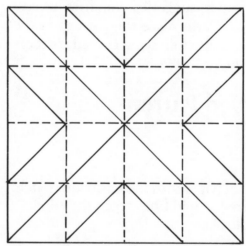

1.

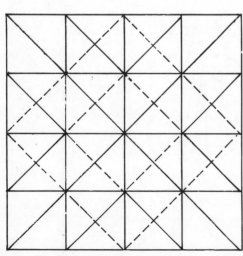

2.

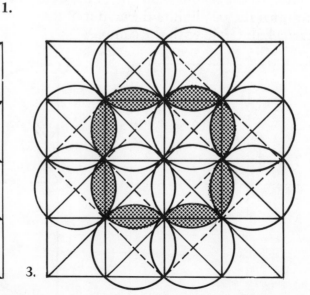

3.

Pullman Puzzle or Baseball

This is another circular pattern based on the four-patch. This time a 64 square grid is needed.

1. Cut out a paper square of the size you need and put a 64 square grid on it.

2. Place the compass on the center of the paper and open it out until it spans two squares crosswise and make a circle.

3. Next with the compass on the same setting, place the point on each of the four corners and make a quarter circle on the paper.

4. Finally, complete the design by ruling across the appropriate squares of the grid to get the design.

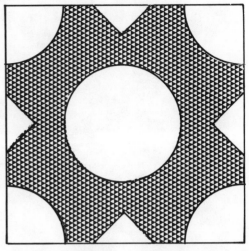

PULLMAN PUZZLE   BASEBALL

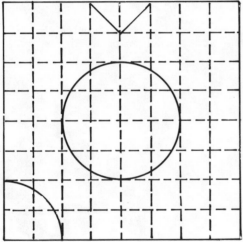

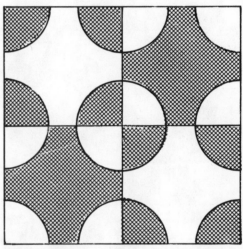

MILL WHEEL

Mill Wheel

Mill Wheel is a repeat pattern of four blocks using the *Rob Peter to Pay Paul* effect, that is, the colors are exactly reversed in opposing units. (See page 158.) A 64 square grid is used for drafting one unit of the design. Four of these units are then put together to form the block.

Place the compass point on each of the four corners of the block and open it out until it spans three small squares along the edge of the block. Make four quarter circles and the design is complete.

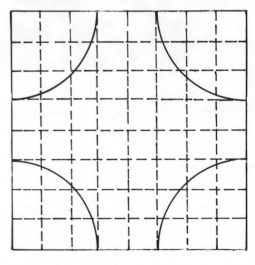

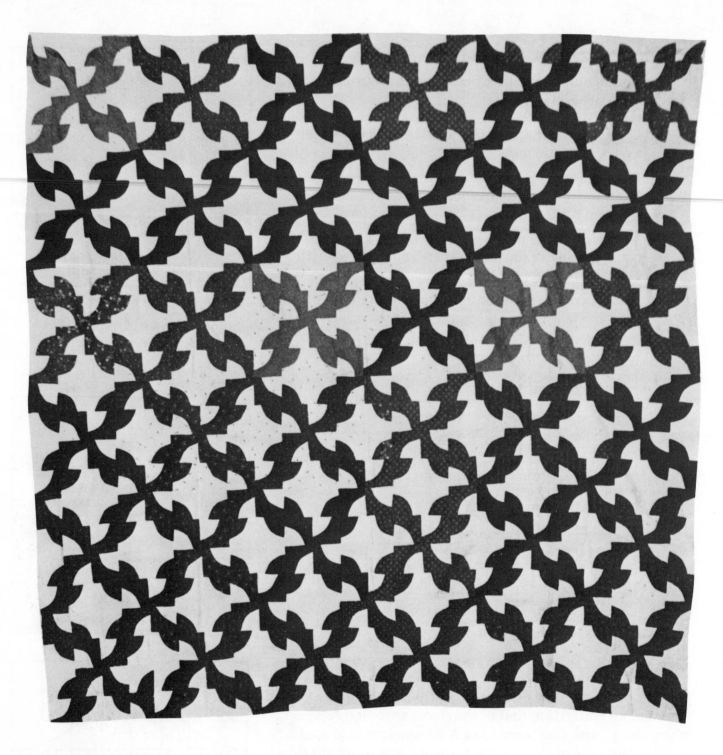

Drunkard's Path. Pieced quilt top from the collection of Dick and Ellen Swanson.

Drunkard's Path

Drunkard's Path is identical to *Mill Wheel* except that the four units of the latter square are not cut apart but used whole while *Drunkard's Path* has the four units cut apart, then put together in many different ways to form squares of such other patterns as *Love Ring, Wonder of the World* and *Fool's Puzzle.* Sometimes the design is pieced so that all quarter circles are the same fabric and all the other pieces another. Sometimes the colors are alternated in a *Robbing Peter to Pay Paul* effect. The designs at right show a few of the variations that can be made with this design.

For both *Mill Wheel* and *Drunkard's Path,* the circle can be made a little larger or smaller. There is no "rule" that says it must be a particular size. However, the proportions used here seem to fit and enhance the structure of the design.

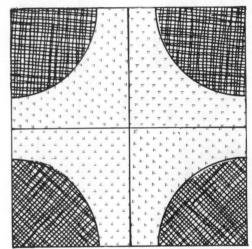

Detail of *Drunkard's Path.*

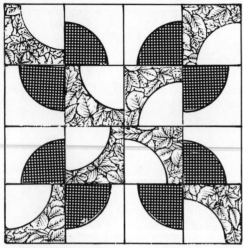

DRUNKARD'S PATH

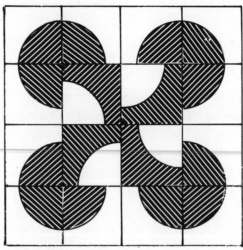

WONDER OF THE WORLD

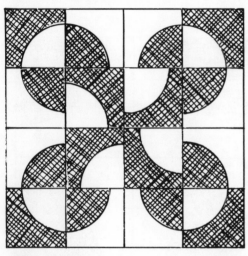

FOOL'S PUZZLE

LOVE RING

Swinging Corners

Swinging Corners is also based on a four-patch grid.

1. Draft a basic four-patch and connect each of the corners of the squares diagonally.

2. Mark the center of each square with a dot (A) and the lines dividing the entire block in half with B.

3. Place the point of the compass on one of the B marks and open it until the pencil reaches an A. Draw a semicircle.

4. Do the same thing at each of the other B points.

5. Next place the point of the compass on each of the four corners and open it until the pencil hits points A. (This will be the same setting on the compass as it was for the semicircles.) Make quarter circles.

Mariner's Compass. Pieced block from wall hanging by Author.

Ray of Light. Detail of pieced medallion quilt by Author.

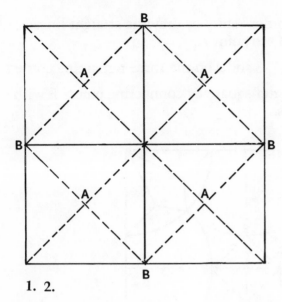

1. 2.

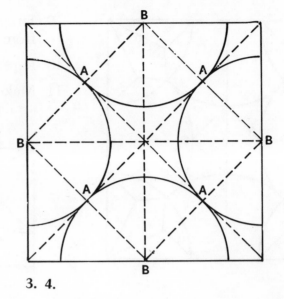

3. 4.

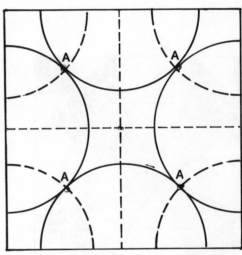

5.

6. Draw straight lines diagonally from one end to the other of each of the four quarter circles.

7. Place a ruler so that it runs from the upper left corner of the block down to point B on the lower edge of the paper. Starting from the corner, draw a line until it reaches the diagonal division across the corner C.

8. Next, keeping one end of the ruler on the same corner, move the other end to the B mark along the right edge of the paper. Again, draw a line until it reaches only the diagonal line C.

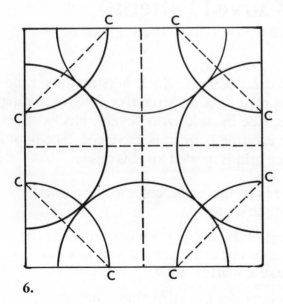

6.

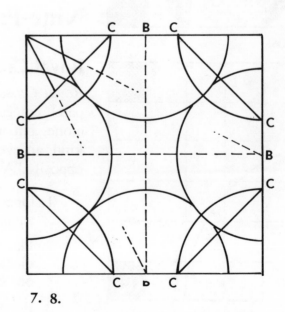

7. 8.

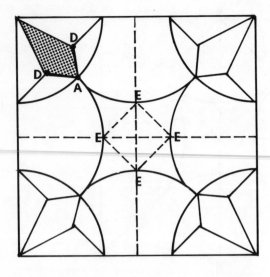

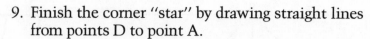

9. Finish the corner "star" by drawing straight lines from points D to point A.

10. Repeat steps 7, 8 and 9 on the three remaining corners.

11. Make the center square by connecting points E with straight lines.

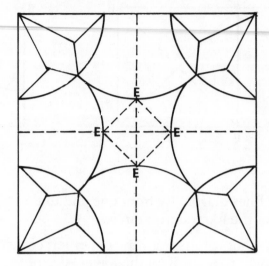

ROYAL CROSS

Nine-Patch Curved Patterns

Royal Cross

Royal Cross is a circular pattern which falls into the nine-patch category. This pattern is an attractive design standing alone, but when set side by side with several blocks of its kind, an even more exciting pattern is produced. (See photo opposite.) A 36 square grid is needed for this design.

1. Once the grid is on the paper, color in the corner squares for the first pieces.

2. Place the point of the compass on one corner of the block and open it out until it spans four blocks along one edge. Make a quarter circle.

3. Repeat the process for the other three corners.

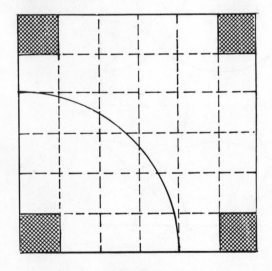

154

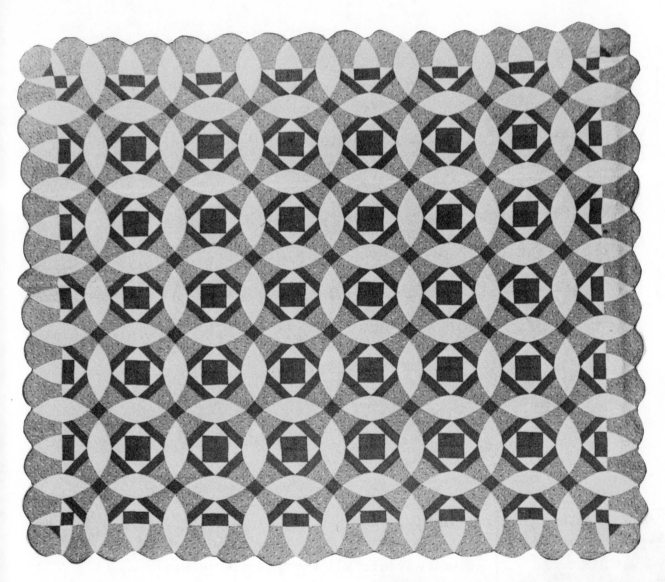

Royal Cross. Circa 1935.

From the collection of Dick and Ellen Swanson.

Detail of *Royal Cross.*

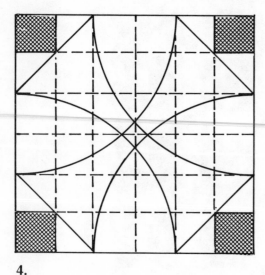

4.

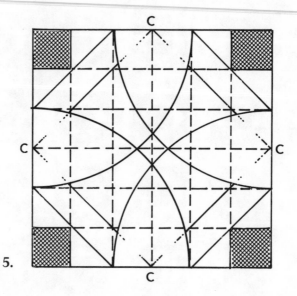

5.

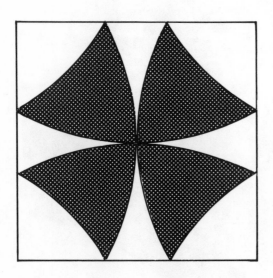

4. Rule diagonally across each of the corner squares of the basic nine-patch.

5. Mark the center folds of the block with C and place the ruler so that it diagonally connects each C with the next. Draw in the portions where the lines fall between the two curves. This will produce the other pieces which form the design.

Winding Ways

Winding Ways is not actually a nine-patch design, but the easiest way to get all the templates is to draft a basic nine-patch grid.

1. Find the center point of each of the nine patches. This can be done by ruling diagonally across the corners of each of the nine squares.

2. Next place the point of the compass in the center of the middle nine-patch square and open it out until the pencil reaches the center of a square directly next to it. Make a circle.

3. Finish the design by placing the compass point in the center of each of the other eight squares and drawing circles in the same manner as before. The center square of the nine-patch will contain one complete unit for the design.

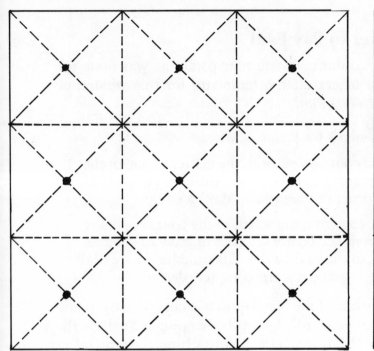

1.

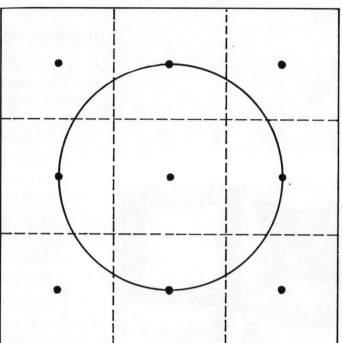

2.

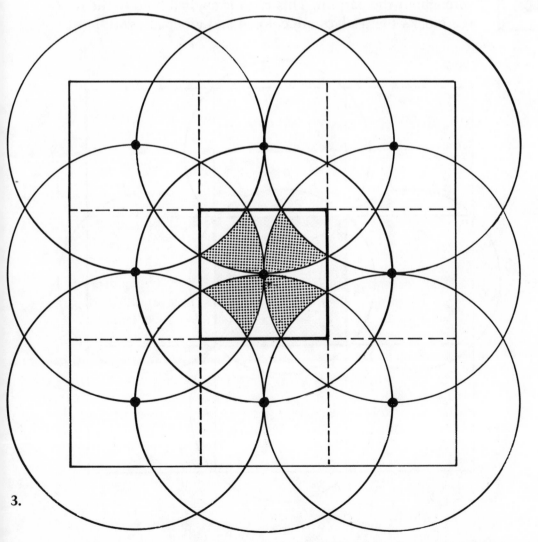

3.

Robbing Peter to Pay Paul

It is necessary to draft a basic nine-patch, as was done for *Winding Ways*, to get all the templates for this version of *Robbing Peter to Pay Paul*.

1. Same as step 1 for *Winding Ways*.

2. Place the compass point in the center of one of the small squares and open it out until the pencil falls on the corner of the square. Make a circle.

3. Without changing the width of the compass, make circles from the centers of each of the four squares adjacent to the middle one. The middle square of the nine-patch will show the complete design.

This is only one of the many quilt patterns with the name *Robbing Peter to Pay Paul*. And still others are said to have the "*Robbing Peter to Pay Paul* effect." In quilting, the term refers to a group of blocks that has one block exactly opposite in coloring to those next to it. The blocks are alternated by color throughout the pattern. This term is applied both to the way the blocks themselves are colored and grouped as well as to

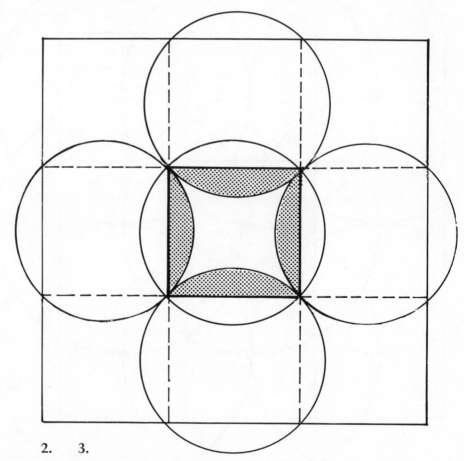

2.   3.

Robbing Peter to Pay Paul. Pieced quilt, circa 1810, from the collection of Mary Ann Shindle.

the way the squares inside each block are colored and grouped. For instance, you could start out with a four-patch of two dark and two light patches. A shape is cut out of a dark square and given to a light square. At the same time the light piece which is displaced is given to the dark square. Alternating blocks in this manner produces some very interesting effects in the overall quilt design.

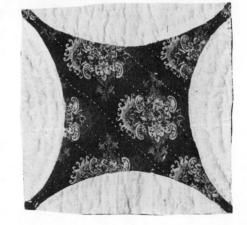

Robbing Peter to Pay Paul. Detail.

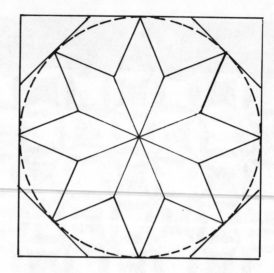

TWINKLING STARS

Eight-Pointed Star Curved Patterns

Twinkling Stars

Twinkling Stars is based on the eight-pointed star. All that is needed is to draft the version of the eight-pointed star on page 99. Put the compass point at the center of the star, open it until it touches one of the points and draw a circle.

The small diamond is drafted in the same way as it was for *Virginia Star* on page 100.

Full Circle Designs Based on "Wedge-Shaped" Divisions of the Circle

Many circular patterns of the *Sunflower* type are based on dividing the circle into a certain number of equal "pie-shaped" wedges. Most of these are created by either dividing the circle first into sixths and then further into 12, 24 or 48 pieces; or dividing the circle into fourths and then further into 8, 16, 32 or 64 pieces. However, there are times when you may want to divide the circle into five or nine divisions or their multiples. Before the ways to make any of the designs are discussed, the ways to divide a circle into the various units will be shown first.

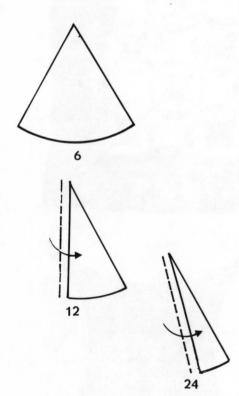

6

12

24

A. A circle divided into sixths.

Follow the first steps for drafting the hexagon page 125. If you wish to have more than six divisions, continue folding the "wedge" in half.

160

B. A circle divided into fourths.

Fold the circle in half to get four divisions and repeat as many times as needed for multiples of four.

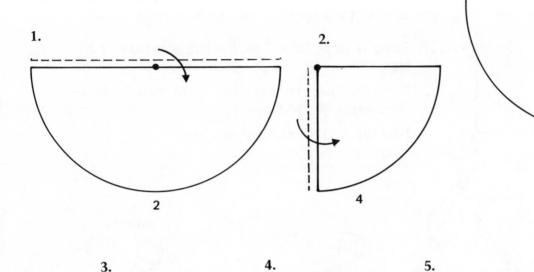

1.

2

2.

4

3.

8

4.

16

5.

32

C. A circle divided into fifths.

The easiest way to divide the circle into fifths is to start with a square, make the divisions first and then draw the circle. It is important to start with a square *larger* than the circle is to be.

1. Fold the paper exactly as for the five-pointed star #1, page 134, steps 1-7. When the paper is opened there will be 10 lines dividing the paper from a central point that is not the center of the paper.

2. Place the compass on the point where the 10 lines intersect and draw the size of circle desired.

3. If a square is needed in which to fit the circle, draft the square from the circle in the method described in Chapter I, page 6.

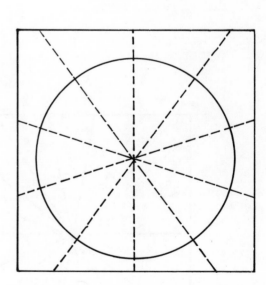

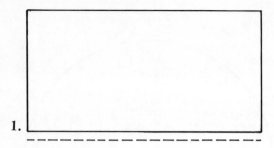

1.

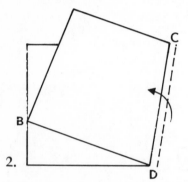

B

1.

D. A circle divided into ninths.

Some versions of the *Sunflower, Dresden Plate* and *Mariner's* designs show the circle divided into 18 divisions. A protractor can be used to mark every 20°, but I have always used the fold method and have had no problem with accuracy. This method is almost identical to the one used in the preceding section for dividing a circle into fifths. Once again, the square used must be larger than the size circle needed and the circle is not cut out of the square until the divisions are made.

1. Same as steps 2 and 3 for the five-pointed star #1, page 134.

2. Bring the lower right corner "A" over to the lower third mark "B" and crease.

3. Fold line CD over to line BD.

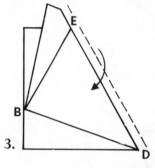

2.

3.

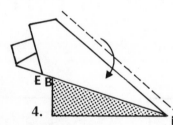

4.

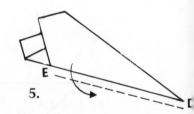

5.

4. Next fold the same section in half again by bringing ED over to BD.

5. Finally, fold the colored area back along BD.

6. When the paper is opened you will find 18 equal divisions.

7. Finish drawing the circle as in Section C, steps 2 and 3.

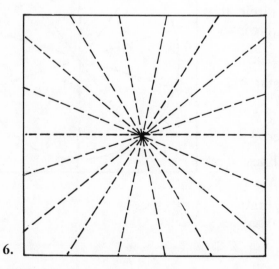

6.

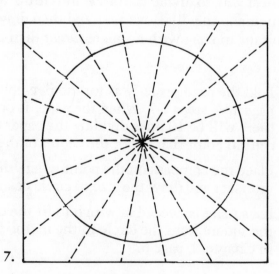

7.

162

When a large number of points are needed, you may feel that there will be some loss of accuracy due to folding the paper so many times. There is another way of dividing the circle into wedges that calls for using a compass and a ruler in very much the same manner that a compass was used to divide a square in Chapter II.

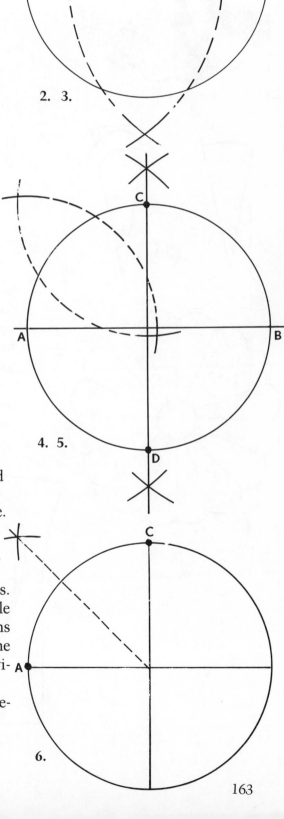

1. Find the center point of the circle and, using a ruler, draw a straight line (AB) from the center through the circumference.

2. Place the point of the compass where the line intersects the circumference (A), open it out larger than the radius and make an arc through line AB.

3. Place the compass on point B and without changing the angle of the compass make two more arcs above and below the line.

4. Connect the points where the two arcs cross with straight lines, and the circle will be divided into fourths.

5. To divide it further, place the compass at point A and make a semicircle. Without changing the setting, place the compass on C and make another semicircle.

6. Again, connect the points where the arcs intersect and extend the line until it meets the circumference.

Repeat the process until the circle is divided into eighths. Using the same process, you can continue dividing the circle into however many units are desired. If you wish divisions for five, six or nine units, it will be necessary to first divide the circle as discussed in sections A, C and D. Then further divisions can be made as described above.

The following are several designs based on "wedge-shaped" divisions of the circle.

163

Dresden Plate

The *Dresden Plate* is a quilt pattern undoubtedly named after Dresden china, a delicate porcelain decorated in bright colors and gold. It was made in Germany from the early 1700's until the late 1800's. The quilt pattern is actually a combination of piecework and applique. To draft it:

1. First draw a circle of whatever size is needed.

2. Decide how many sections the plate will have. Ordinarily there are 16, 18 or 20 divisions. Using one of the fold methods described above, divide the circle into the number of units you wish to have.

3. Once it is folded, "scallop" the edge using a compass, spool or other round object and cut off the excess. Cut off the center tip.

4. Open the paper. Cut out one of the sections for the template.

   When all the divisions are pieced, the "plate" is then appliqued to a square. A circle larger than the middle opening is appliqued to the center of the plate.

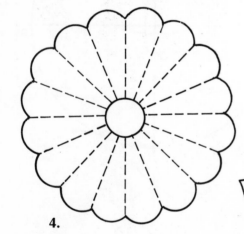

Most full circle patterns are *pieced* into a square as opposed to being appliqued onto it as in the *Dresden Plate*. Contrary to what many believe, piecing the circle produces both sharper points and a much more even and smooth effect. In order to achieve this, when you draw a circle and cut it out to make a design, *save* the rest of the square from which the circle was cut. I usually divide that piece into fourths and save one quarter section to use as a template for the outside of the circle.

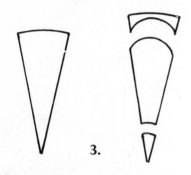

3.

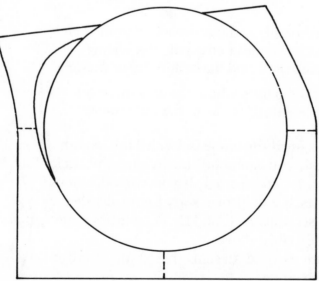

4.

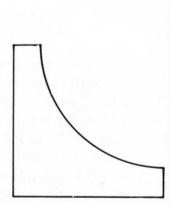

It is easier and neater to fit four sections around the circle than to try to fit the circle into a "hole." Don't forget that the seam allowances will have to be added to that template just as they must be added to all other pattern pieces.

Grandmother's Fan

Most of the fan designs can be made in much the same manner as *Dresden Plate*. The only difference is that, instead of drafting the entire circle, a quarter circle is drawn in one corner of a square. The quarter circle is then cut out and folded into however many divisions are required. A smaller quarter circle is drawn to form the center of the fan.

Wheel of Fortune

Wheel of Fortune is an easy design to draft. Draw the size of square needed and make a circle which almost fills the square. Make a small circle in the middle and then a larger circle with a radius about three-quarters of the radius of the larger circle. (There is no set distance between the circles. Make the proportions whatever you wish.) Next cut the circle out and fold it to get 16 divisions.

Indian Summer

Indian Summer is not as complicated to draft as it may look.

1. Cut a square of paper, fold it into a four-patch and then crease it diagonally from corner to corner.

2. Place the compass on each of the four corners and open it out until the pencil reaches the fold line which divides the square in half, and make quarter circles.

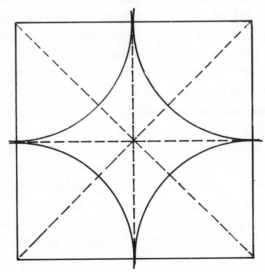

1. 2.

GRANDMOTHER'S FAN

WHEEL OF FORTUNE

INDIAN SUMMER

165

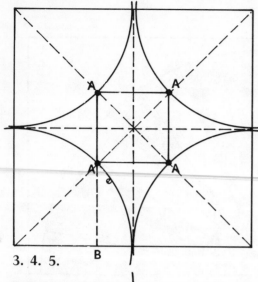

3. 4. 5.

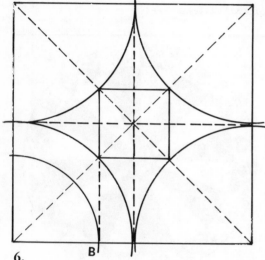

6.

VARIATION I

3. Next make a dot (A) where the circles touch the diagonal fold lines.

4. Connect points A to get the center square.

5. Extend the left side of the center square to the lower edge of the block and mark point B.

6. Place the compass point on the lower left corner and open it out to point B and make another quarter circle from B.

7. Cut out one of the large quarter circle sections and fold it into sixteenths.

8. Open the paper. With a ruler and a pencil make the "sawtooth" edge by drawing diagonally up from the edge of the paper at the inner circle point to where the first fold line touches the outer edge of the circle, and then down to the inner circle again as in the diagram below.

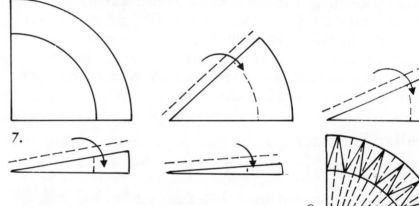

7.

8.

Mariner's Compass and Sunflower Designs

There are many variations of *Mariner's Compass, Blazing Star* or *Sunflower*. The number of points may vary; the points may be thick or thin; there may be a circle, star or other design in the center. A few basic designs will be shown here with some suggestions on how they can be changed to give other effects. Each of these designs has been called a variety of names and the patterns are easily altered; so, if you choose to use one, you should name it whatever you like that suits the mood of your quilt.

The description below will show how to get a design with three layers of points; that is, there are three different sized points which give the effect of overlapping each other. The majority of these types of designs are either based on multiples of six points (12, 24 or 48) or multiples of eight points (16 or 32). Depending on the size of the block and on how

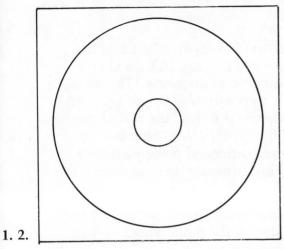

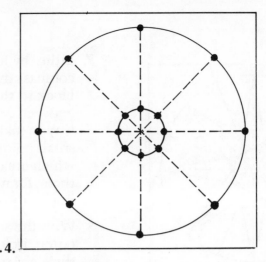

1. 2.   **3. 4.**

complex you wish it to be, you can either stop after making a few points or keep going to get as many as you wish. The method described here is based on eight points, but it is exactly the same procedure used for six. The only change is how the paper is divided at the beginning. To make drafting this design easier, use three different colored pens and/or pencils.

Variation I

1. Draw a circle the size you wish with a compass. If you can't make a circle big enough with the compass, try tracing around a large plate or other round object.

2. Find the center of the circle. (If you used a plate or other large object, fold the circle in quarters to find the center.) Make a small circle with the compass.

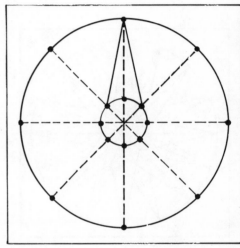

5.

Note: There is no "set" size for this center circle. You will need to experiment to find the proportions you like best. *However*, the smaller the circle, the thinner the points of the star will be and the larger the circle, the fatter the points will be.

3. Next cut the circle out and fold it into eighths (Section B, steps 1 through 3, page 161).

4. Open the circle, take the first colored pencil and make two dots on each fold line: One at the outer edge and the other at the point where the fold line touches the inner circle.

5. Place the ruler on one of the outer dots and angle it sideways until it hits the dot on the inner circle on the next fold line and draw a line connecting the dots. Working from the same dot, angle the ruler to the inner dot on the fold line on the other side and draw another line.

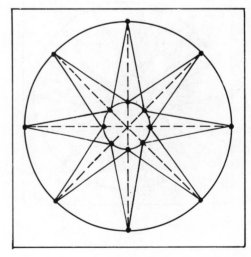

6.

6. Repeat the process seven more times to get the first eight points of the design.

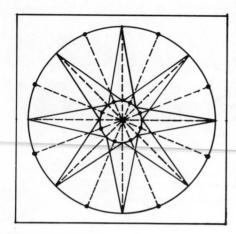

7. 8.

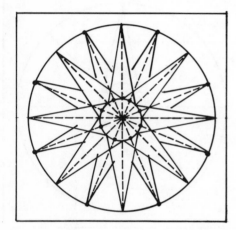

9.

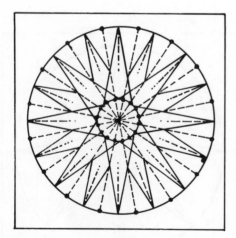

9.

7. Either by folding (Section B, step 4) or by using the compass method described on page 163, divide the block so that there are now 16 divisions. (The distance between each point has been divided in half.) A third way to make the divisions is to find the tips of the small points around the center circle. Find two tips which are opposite each other and place a ruler on them. Draw a line connecting the tips and extend the line to the edges of the circle.

8. With the second colored pencil make one dot on the outer circle and one dot on the inner where each of the eight new folds cross them.

9. Once again angle the ruler from the new outer dots to the adjacent inner dots of the same color and make lines. It is important to note that you do not draw the whole line. Stop when you get to the edges of the first eight points. The second group of points will thus have the effect of "lying under" the first.

10. Again, using whichever of the three methods you prefer, divide the circle so that there will now be 32 divisions.

11. With the third colored pencil make a third set of dots along the outer and inner circles where they are bisected by each of the new folds. This time there will be 16 new folds.

12. Place the ruler on one of the new outer dots and again angle it toward the inner circle, but this time *skip* the usual adjacent dot of the new color and go to the next one of that color. If you fail to do this, the last set of points will not have the same angle as the others. Again, do not extend the line clear to the inner circle. Stop when it touches another triangle.

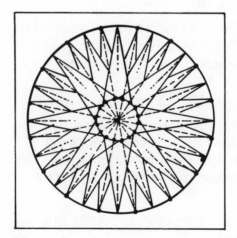

10.

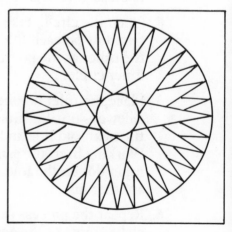

12.

Variation II

If you wish the compass to look like *Variation II*, put the point of the compass on the center of the circle and open it until it reaches the place where the second set of points meet the first set. Draw a circle. (Only that portion of the circle which cuts across the bottom of the second set of points will be used.) Do the same with the third set of points.

VARIATION II

Variation III

Blazing Star, Blazing Sun, Sunflower 1

Blazing Star and *Sunflower* are exactly the same except for the size of the center circle. Two totally different effects can thus be achieved with one change.

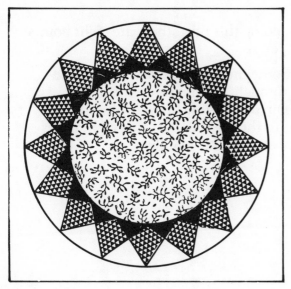

SUNFLOWER

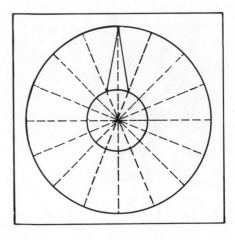

BLAZING STAR   BLAZING SUN

The drafting of this pattern is almost identical to that of *Variation I* above, but this time all the folds in the circle are made at the beginning.

1. and 2. Same as steps 1 and 2 in *Variation I* above.

3. Divide the circle so there are 16 divisions.

4. Starting where one fold intersects the center circle, rule diagonally upward to where the next fold crosses the outer circle. Angle the ruler down again to the next fold and draw another line.

3. 4.

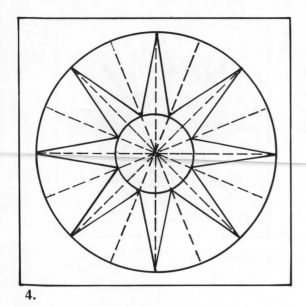

4.

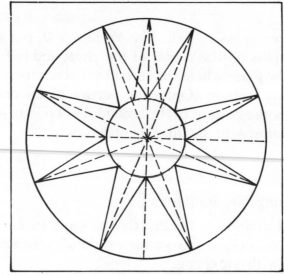

5.

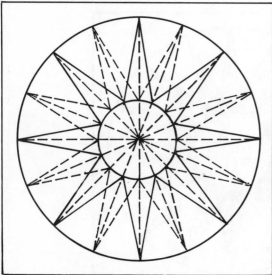

5.

Continue doing this until there are eight points on the paper.

5. Starting from where a fold bisects the circle and cuts through the middle of one of the points, again draw a line up to the next fold and down to the next. Repeat this eight times and the design will be complete.

Variation IV

This variation uses the same concept as the previous methods, but more circles are added. You can continue drawing as many circles as you want and adding points to get a "Chrysanthemum" effect.

1. Draw four circles on the paper—one the size of the design, another one within that, a smaller one inside that, and a still smaller center circle.

2. Ignoring the outer circle and working with the next two inner circles as if they were the total area of the design, draft the pattern exactly as you have done for *Variation III.*

VARIATION IV

170

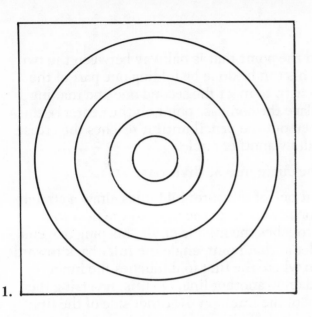

1.

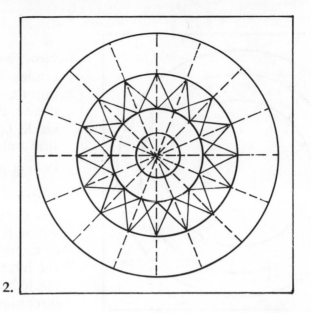

2.

3. Divide the circle one more time so there are 32 divisions.

4. Working from a fold which touches the tip of one of the points of the inner design, draw lines up to the next fold and down to the next around the circle to complete the design in the outer circle. Following the diagram use the new folds to make the inner points.

Variation V—Sunflower 2

Most of the *Sunflower* patterns have very large center circles. To draft a basic *Sunflower:*

1. Draw the first circle as large as you want the entire design to be.

2. Draw a "fat" center circle.

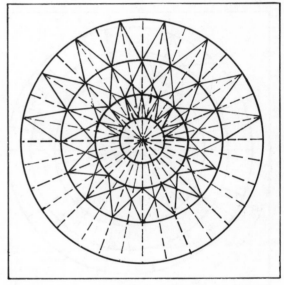

3. 4.

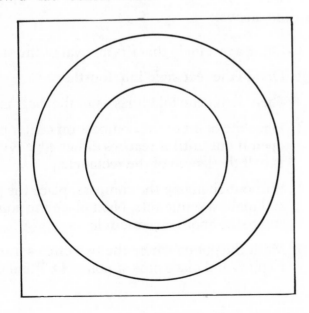

SUNFLOWER 2

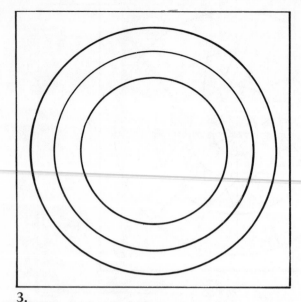

3.

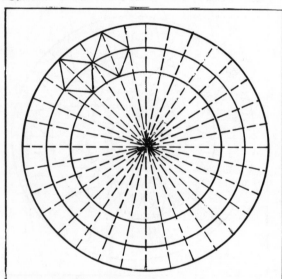

4. 5. 6.

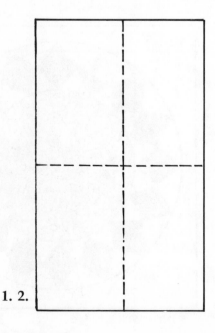

1. 2.

3. Now find the point that is halfway between the two circles. This can be done by folding one part of the outer circle in to meet the second one and making a crease. Place the compass point on the center of the circle, open out the pencil until it reaches the crease line and draw another circle.

4. Divide the circle into 32 divisions.

5. Starting at one of the outer fold lines, draw a straight line diagonally down to the right to the next fold where it touches the middle circle. Keeping one end of the ruler at that point, angle the ruler back towards the left to where the first fold touches the inner circle and draw another line. Do this, reversing the directions of the lines, on the other side of the first fold line to make a diamond shape.

6. Continue until 16 "diamonds" have been made around the circle.

There are hundreds of circular designs which can be made in the same manner as the designs described above. Among other possibilities, variations in the size of the circles, the number of divisions and placement of the lines can make total changes in the design.

Oval Designs

The same concepts can also be used in oval motifs. Many times an elongated design is desired for the center of a medallion quilt or for a wall hanging. The oval can be folded in the same manner as the circle to get equal divisions.

To draft an oval:

1. Draw a rectangle that fits an oval of the size you wish.

2. Divide the rectangle into fourths.

   Then, letter the fold lines as in the diagram.

3. Place the point of the compass on center point C and open it out until it reaches either edge A or B. (This is half the length of the rectangle.)

4. Without changing the compass, place the point on D and make a semicircle. Next place the point on E and make another semicircle.

5. Mark the points where the two circles intersect with F and G and place pins at points D, F and G.

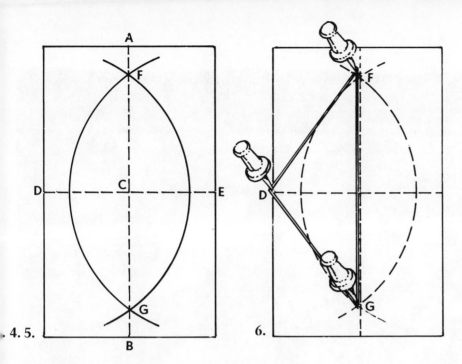

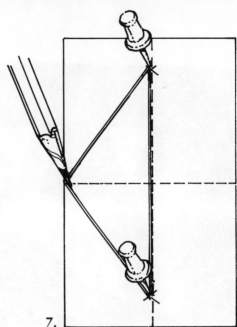

4. 5.

6.

7.

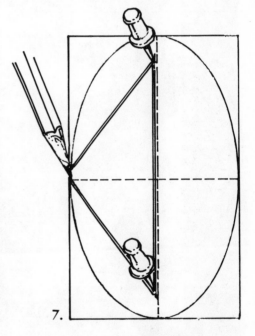

6. Tie a string around the three pins tightly enough so that there is no slack.

7. Remove pin D and put a pencil in its place. Keeping the string taut, pull the pencil around the pins to draw the oval.

Any of the circular sunflower patterns can be drafted in an oval in the same manner as they were in a circle. For example, take an oval and divide it into 16 divisions. Make a smaller center oval by constructing a small rectangle inside the oval and following steps 2-7 above.

Make the points exactly as you did for *Variation III.* You will notice that the thickness of the points varies around the oval. Therefore more templates are needed—five for the large points, four for the small points and four "filler" pieces. These templates are reversed for each of the three remaining quarters of the design.

7.

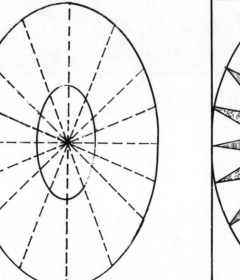

173

Facets. Pieced quilt based on the *Kaleidoscope.* By
Susan McKelvey.

CHAPTER XII

Original Design

When thinking about "original" geometric design, the question is: What *is* original? How can one say a pattern has never been used before? I feel that when working in a structured area such as that of geometric motifs, it is very difficult to create a totally "original" design. There is only so much that can be done with the divisions of a square, circle, rectangle or other geometric shape. One may arrive at an idea that is original to him or her, but two weeks later that person may see the same design in a book. *Inner City*, page 128, was my "original" design, but after I started the quilt I found a similar motif depicted in two different sources. Whenever anyone asks me if my work is original, I am quick to point out that although it may be "original" with me, I cannot say that there is not another like it or that I designed it "first." Originality and innovation in geometric quilt design lies more in the placement of blocks, the size of units, the type of borders and the interaction of color and fabric than in devising a design motif which has never been used before.

Study of ancient geometric motifs, particularly those from the Middle East and Asia, shows hundreds of geometric patterns identical to those we use in our quilts today. The apparent duplication of patterns does not mean that modern quiltmakers copied those motifs; instead, it demonstrates that when any society starts experimenting with similar ideas, like conclusions are apt to occur. All of history is built on what has gone before. We learn from the past and build on it for even greater ideas.

A Dover book entitled *Japanese Design Motifs* contains more than 4,000 ancient Japanese patterns. I have drawn some here that are identical to some of our quilt patterns today. The names have been translated into English.

Even with the knowledge that most geometric motifs have probably been made by someone somewhere in the

BOBBINS

CHRYSANTHEMUM

WINDMILL

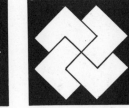

FOUR PLAYING STONES

NINE STONES
CONNECTING

world, it is still exciting to experiment and come up with a design that is new to you. There are versions of geometric designs and geometric combinations as well as color and fabric use that can create a totally new look in a quilt design. It is more exciting to create your own than to make an exact copy of someone else's quilt. I have designed several "original" patterns throughout the book, mainly for the chapter on five-pointed stars and for this chapter. I have developed these patterns to help you to understand the guidelines for designing, as well as in the hope that it will spur you to try creating some of your own.

Many people think that they cannot be creative and that they *must* copy a quilt design or use a traditional block to make a good quilt. Before I started quilting I used to feel that way about the things I made. I am thankful that I became interested in quilting when I was living in India. There, I was totally isolated from other quilters and *had* to do things the way *I* felt they should be done, not the way they were "supposed" to be done. As a result, I embarked unwittingly on a color and fabric system that was, in large, not being used in quiltmaking at that time. Because of my isolation I was able to express my own ideas. I am sure that had I been in this country I would have looked through books and studied quilts, and thus would have known how quilts are "supposed" to be made. I would then have believed that I did not have the ability to produce anything as "good" as those that I had seen. Therefore, I would have felt the need to copy as I had copied other handwork in my pre-quilting days.

I grew up feeling very inadequate about my ability to *create* something different. My mother and sister were the artists in the family and I could not possibly compete with them. Perhaps I had a sort of middle-child syndrome. But we all have to break out of our shells one day and say, "I am worth something, I can create," and most of all, "I have confidence in myself and in my ability to do something different." That day came for me when I returned to the United States with my first, and, to me, not extraordinary, quilt top. People raved about how beautiful the quilt was, what a sense of color I had, and how different my rendition of *Grandmother's Flower Garden* was. Suddenly, I began to feel confident that I *could* do something different, that I did not have to copy another person's ideas, and that perhaps I could also put some of my own ideas to use in helping others.

The most important thing of all is not to be discouraged by failures. We all make mistakes: Our designs don't turn out the way we thought they would and the fabrics that looked so great when they were spread out on the floor may look terrible when made up into the block. Only by persisting can you create something which you are proud of and which is truly your own.

We tend to think that artists get a "vision" and put it down on canvas or patch it in fabric. However, many times creation involves a long process of continual thought and work from the beginning idea to the finished product. At other times an artist may finish an abstract piece and then turn it in every direction until he finds the best angle.

Creating new quilts and designs requires *time,* and sometimes finding that time is the most difficult task of all. I try hard to make time because I feel it is important to me as a person to do something creative. I set aside every evening after dinner to work on my quilts. This is a time when I can relax with my family. If the laundry is not finished or if other work needs to be done, I feel that it can wait until tomorrow. My house is not immaculate, but I think it is more important to me as a person to quilt than it is to keep the cobwebs out of the rafters. In addition to my evenings, I try to steal whatever bits of time I can. I keep sewing by the phone for those long-winded conversations, or for when I have to wait forever on hold. I take handwork to doctors' offices, Little League games and when I ride in the car. However, planning a new quilt or working a new design requires more concentrated effort than the mere snatches of time one can find. Once a year I set aside one full week to start a new quilt. Many people get the doldrums after Christmas. After all the general excitement and the hustle, bustle and hurrying to get last minute projects done, many times the day after Christmas is a letdown. Not for me. That is my time to plan and design a new quilt. All year I have had ideas forming in my head about what I might like to do and I have been beginning to get ideas about fabrics and colors. Therefore, I look forward to the week after Christmas when I can devote a huge block of time to planning something personally exciting.

When planning a new project, I do not graph the whole quilt ahead of time. I believe a quilt has to "grow" as I sew it. How can I tell what border or setting strip is going to look best until I have laid it out and have tried different possibilities? There is a big difference between the colors of pencils and those of fabrics. A design might look beautiful when colored in pencil on paper, but a whole new dimension is added by the interplay of the prints in the fabric. Fabrics may look great laid out next to each other but when cut and pieced in a design, they take on dramatically different aspects.

Of course, a basic outline is necessary. I decide on the size of block I want and usually on the size of the borders. I also gather a carefully selected group of fabrics that I am interested in using, but I determine which fabrics I will use in a specific spot and what border designs will look best when I get to them. Certainly most painters do not make a chart on graph paper or some other "painting by numbers" arrangement before starting their work. They may have a basic outline of the shapes they want to emphasize, but they add colors and textures as needed.

Many people then ask, "If I don't know what I'm going to use where, how much fabric should I buy?" It is difficult to say how much material to buy, but I feel that two of my best successes in quiltmaking were due to running out of fabric and having to use what was available. It puts your mind to work and instead of doing the "ordinary" you are forced to come up with solutions you might never have thought of.

When doing a "block" quilt, I enjoy making all the blocks first and then arranging and rearranging them to find different design possibilities. Sometimes it means leaving the blocks laid out on the floor for a week and trying to get a new perspective on them each time I enter the room. Other times it means making new blocks, or redoing some to get a color that is needed. I will usually invite a friend in to get her ideas —I find it really helps to discuss projects with other people. They can give you ideas which in turn spark more of yours and out of these a really exciting synthesis can emerge.

I ask my family over and over, "How does this look?" They are usually quite good about telling me just what they see, until I have gone overboard with my questions and then I hear, "I already told you a hundred times, it looks great!"

I once made a crazy quilt with lots of elaborate embroidery and had all the blocks laid out trying to arrive at a good placement of them. I was quite proud of a spiderweb I had embroidered and had it placed in a prominent spot in the center of the quilt where it would readily be seen. I asked each family member in turn how the layout looked and each took a fleeting glance and said, "Fine." Then my son, who was ten at the time, came along and really studied the blocks. Finally he said, "It all looks great except for the spiderweb. If you ever see a spiderweb in a room it is always in the corner, and this one should be in the corner of your quilt."

I feel that if I graph everything out ahead of time, I do not leave myself open for change or flexibility. By mechanically following a diagram I would deprive myself of the joy of discovery.

Guidelines for Original Designs

The preceding chapters have given in detail the drafting methods for the various categories of geometric design. These same methods can be used as a basis for creating new design motifs. I will try here to present various guidelines for developing some original patterns.

Folding One Category on Another

Perhaps one of the most interesting ways to create new patterns is through repeatedly folding the paper. You have seen how, in the drafting methods of the various categories, it is possible to make many different designs depending on which fold lines are colored in. It is fun just to start folding the paper into a four-patch perhaps and then diagonally and diagonally again. Make however many folds you like and then open the paper to see what you have. You can also draft one category on top of another, but when experimenting with new designs I find it best to use the fold methods for the various categories. There is no need to worry about accuracy when experimenting—the pattern can be redrafted with care once you have decided which version to use. With folding, more design possibilities occur because there are more lines on the paper. After folding two categories on the same square, open the paper, hold it at an angle to the light and squint. The folds on the paper and the way the light shines on them from various angles will cause different designs to jump out.

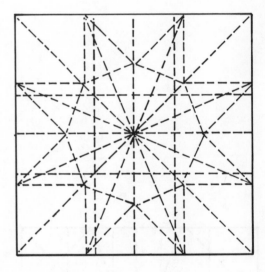

Design 1

This design was made by folding a square of paper into a nine-patch and then opening it and folding it into an eight-pointed star. Certain folds were colored in to achieve the design.

Design 2

Design 2 is created from the folds formed when a 16 square four-patch is folded on top of a kaleidoscope.

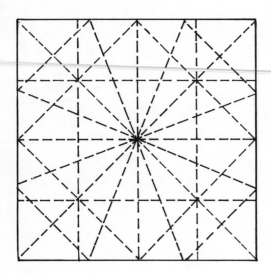

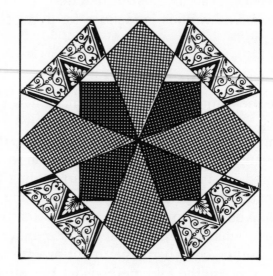

Design 3

This design is a combination of a kaleidoscope folded on top of a five-patch grid.

The motifs which I have designed for this chapter are presented as guides in the hope that you will experiment further with all the various fold methods and develop some of your own motifs. You might even try imposing three grids on top of each other.

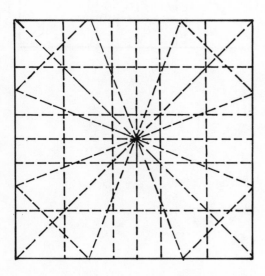

Setting the Blocks Together

Once you have experimented with the folds of the block and have come up with a design you would like to try, there are various ways of arranging the blocks within a quilt.

The first consideration is how the blocks are set together. Perhaps the least interesting way of setting them is with lattice strips separating each block. With this type of setting the block maintains its identity as an individual unit.

A second possibility is alternating pieced blocks with plain blocks. Once again the blocks will change very little in appearance. Blocks can be either set squarely or diagonally.

A third setting method is to place the blocks side by side. This presents the greatest opportunity for interaction of the design elements and for the formation of secondary designs over the surface of the quilt. For example, look at designs 1, 2 and 3 on the previous pages, and then see on the following pages how much more interesting they become when several of the units are placed side by side.

The blocks can also be varied by alternating their coloring in different ways. One way is to make half of all the blocks the exact opposite of the other half in coloring and then alternate them as is done in the *Rob Peter to Pay Paul* effect. Another way is to vary the colors within certain blocks and play with the arrangement. This is illustrated in the quilt pictured on page 174. The design is the basic kaleidoscope, but by varying the color placement, a totally different design emerges. Another example is the wall hanging on page 185. This is made simply of triangles sewn together, but by color and fabric variation an exciting design comes forth.

Deciding on the set, placement and coloring of the blocks can be time consuming, particularly if you wish to experiment and see the possibilities for various designs before actually cutting and piecing. It is impossible to judge the interaction of the blocks unless you have several units to play with. A lot of time can be saved by drawing one or more of the motifs on a piece of paper and then making several photocopies. The blocks can then be cut out, colored in and arranged and rearranged until you find a placement that appeals to you. Artist's spray adhesive is excellent to use for experimenting with placement. The backs of the units can be sprayed and then they can be arranged on a piece of cardboard. With the adhesive they can be picked up and put back down as many times as you wish. The cardboard can be propped up so that the design can be viewed from a distance without the small pieces of paper falling all over the place.

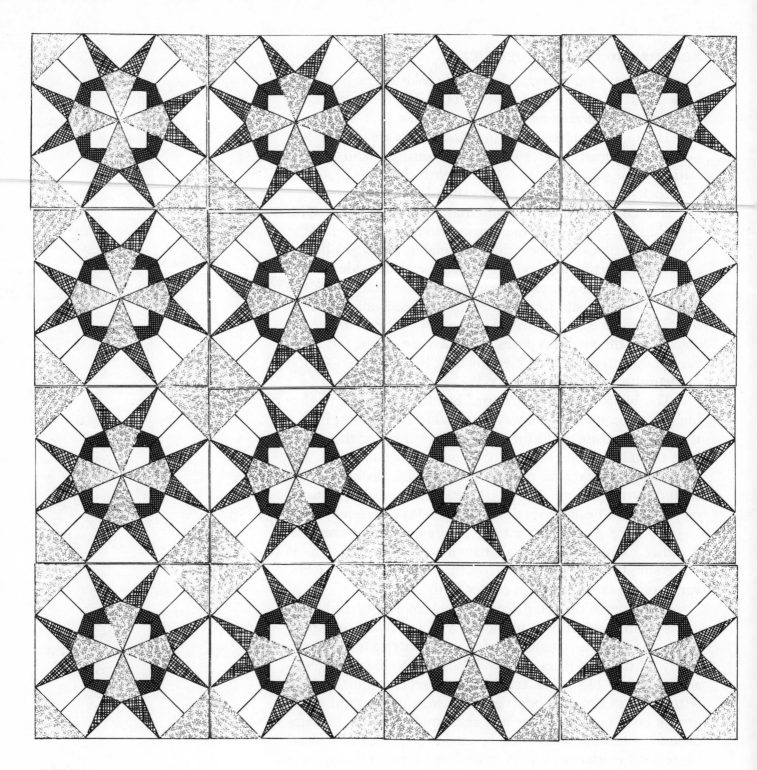

DESIGN 1

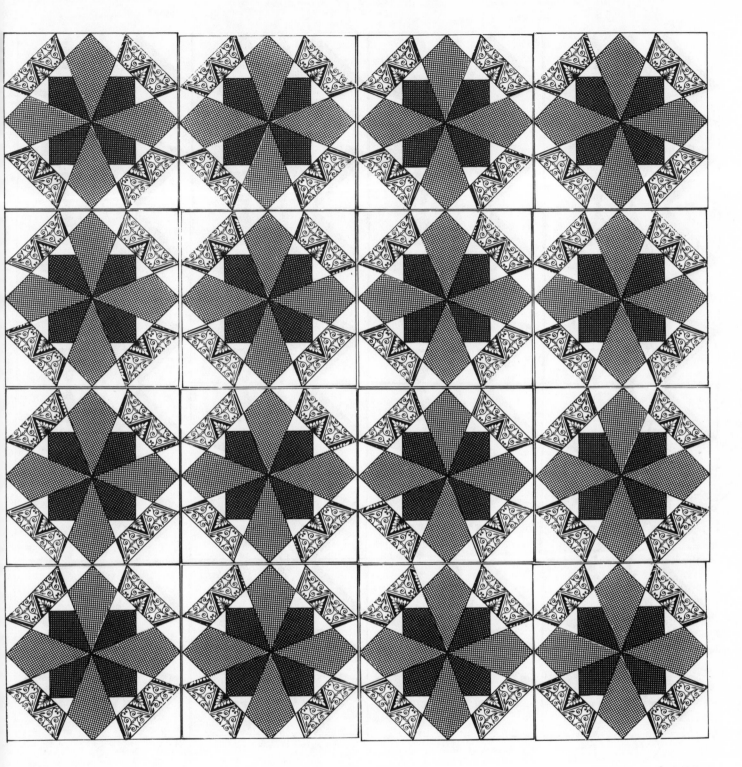

DESIGN 2

183

DESIGN 3

Star Rise. Pieced wall hanging by Barbara Bockman.

MEXICAN CROSS   MEXICAN ROSE

Alternating Blocks

Another possibility for innovation in quilt design is alternating two compatible blocks in the design. It is most exciting to use your own original designs. However, numerous possibilities exist employing traditional motifs. The best balance of design usually occurs when two motifs from the same category are combined. For example, the *Mexican Cross* and the following variation of the kaleidoscope are both in the eight-pointed star category. When they are alternated in an overall design, a totally new image emerges.

Another design based on putting two different blocks together is the following one where *Mexican Cross* and *Castle Wall* have been alternated.

CASTLE WALL

By using a variety of colors and fabrics there are even more possibilities for unusual effects. Draft two designs from the same category that appeal to you and try different combinations of tones and textures. If you judiciously alternate patterns from various categories, you should be able to develop some lovely quilt designs that have perhaps never been used before.

MEXICAN ROSE and CASTLE WALL

187

Rearranging a Block

Another way to experiment with design is to take a traditional or original block, divide it and put it back together in a different way. For example, draft the basic eight-pointed star. To make it more interesting, make diagonal lines across the corners.

Cut it into quarters and put it back together with two corners of the original star pointing in and two pointing out, as in the diagram below.

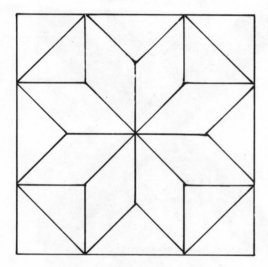

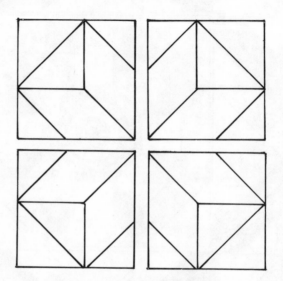

The unit by itself is not particularly interesting, but when several blocks are put together, a design more exciting than the basic star is seen. Any block can be cut up and reorganized in this manner. The variations and possibilities are endless.

EIGHT-POINTED STAR — REARRANGED

BACHELOR'S PUZZLE

MEXICAN STAR

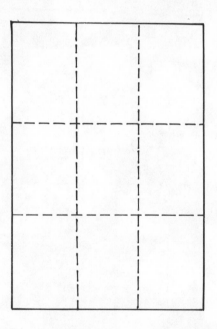

Rectangle

An area of quilt design which has, in large, not been explored is that of rectangular design. The same concepts that apply to squares can also be applied to rectangles and similar designs can be used. The rectangle can be divided into a "grid" just as a square can be. The effect will be that of *elongating* the design. For example, a rectangle divided into a nine-patch "grid" would look like this:

The width is folded into thirds and then the length is folded into thirds. Another way of making the grid is to use a ruler as described in Chapter III to make the divisions. A rectangle has been used as a basis for the designs at left. They are the same patterns that have been described in previous chapters except that here they have been drawn on a rectangular grid.

These blocks also look very different when placed side by side, as can be seen in the following diagrams of *Nine-Patch Kaleidoscope* and *Air Castle*.

OHIO STAR

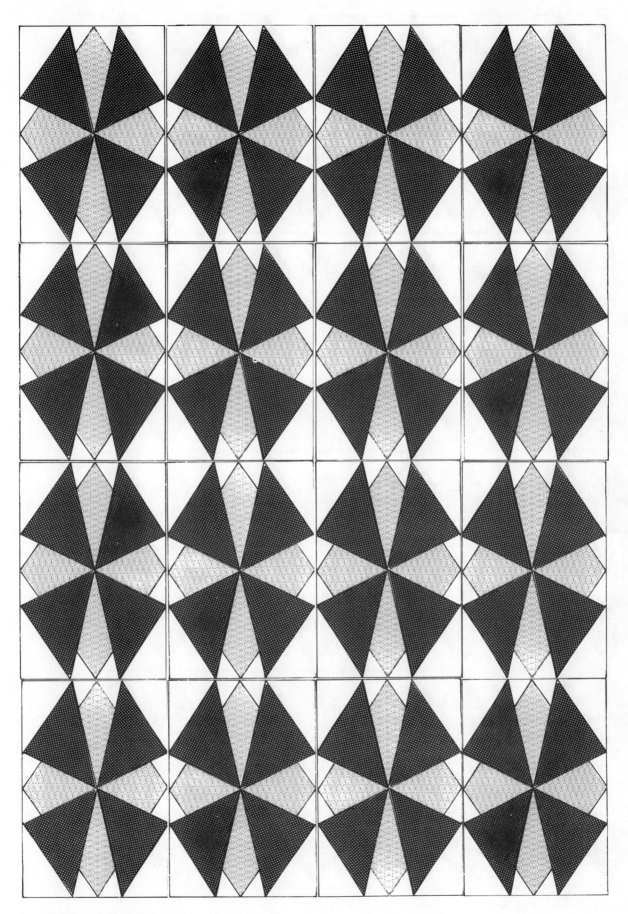

NINE-PATCH KALEIDOSCOPE

191

AIR CASTLE

Now that you have seen how easy it is to make geometric designs, let your imagination go. A work of art requires creativity. It also, of course, requires labor; but, as I sew, I relax and enjoy a feeling of tranquility all too rare in the modern world. The excitement of designing a quilt and the quiet hours devoted to making something that has a lifetime longer than my own give me profound pleasure. It is this joy that I wish most of all that you may share with me.

Category Test

(1) CHEVRON

(2) ROLLING STAR

(3) CROSS AND CROWN

(4) TWIN SISTERS

(5) BOX QUILT

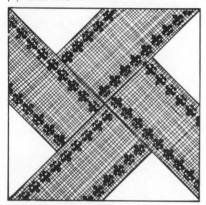

(6) BACHELOR'S PUZZLE

(7) CASTLE WALL

(8) EVENING STAR

(9) QUEEN CHARLOTTE'S CROWN

(10) PALM LEAF

(11) AUNT SUKEY'S CHOICE

(12) GENTLEMAN'S FANCY

The following blocks are a sample of the patterns in the book. See if you can place them in their proper category. Look on page 196 for the answers.

(13) INDIAN TRAIL

(14) BACHELOR'S PUZZLE

(15) GRANDMOTHER'S CROSS

(16) TRIANGLES AND STRIPES

(17) ODD FELLOWS PATCH

(18) SPIDERWEB

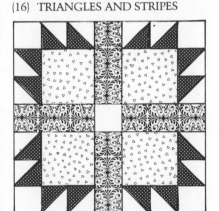

(19) BEAR'S PAW

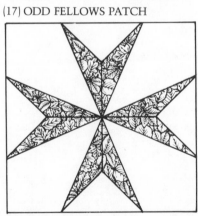

(20) V BLOCK

(21) CENTENNIAL

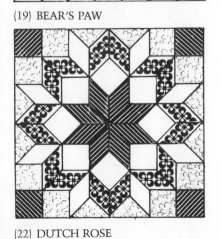

(22) DUTCH ROSE

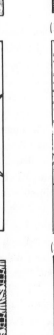

(23) TALL PINE TREE

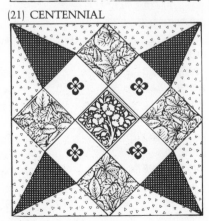

(24) SKY ROCKET

1. *CHEVRON*   Four-Patch
2. *ROLLING STAR*   Eight-Pointed Star
3. *CROSS AND CROWN*   Five-Patch
4. *TWIN SISTERS*   Four-Patch
5. *BOX QUILT*   Nine-Patch
6. *BACHELOR'S PUZZLE*   Five-Patch
7. *CASTLE WALL*   Eight-Pointed Star
8. *EVENING STAR*   Eight-Pointed Star
9. *QUEEN CHARLOTTE'S CROWN*   Five-Patch
10. *PALM LEAF*   Four-Patch
11. *AUNT SUKEY'S CHOICE*   Nine-Patch
12. *GENTLEMAN'S FANCY*   Nine-Patch
13. *INDIAN TRAIL*   Four-Patch
14. *BACHELOR'S PUZZLE*   Four-Patch
15. *GRANDMOTHER'S CROSS*   Five-Patch
16. *TRIANGLE AND SQUARES*   Four-Patch
17. *ODDFELLOWS PATCH*   Five-Patch
18. *SPIDERWEB*   Eight-Pointed Star
19. *BEAR'S PAW*   Seven-Patch
20. *V BLOCK*   Eight-Pointed Star
21. *CENTENNIAL*   Four-Patch
22. *DUTCH ROSE*   Eight-Pointed Star
23. *TALL PINE TREE*   Five-Patch
24. *SKY ROCKET*   Nine-Patch

Index

199

Drawing by Wendy Kahle.